AUTOMATION OF LIBRARY INTEGRATED OPERATIONS
A How to do Manual

AUTOMATION OF LIBRARY INTEGRATED OPERATIONS

A How to do Manual

By
V. Uma
V.J. Suseela

Ess Ess Publications
New Delhi

AUTOMATION OF LIBRARY INTEGRATED OPERATIONS
A How to do Manual

ISBN: 978-81-933597-2-3

First Published 2017

Published by:
Ess Ess Publications
4831/24, Ansari Road,
Darya Ganj,
New Delhi-110 002.
INDIA
Phones: 23260807, 41563444
Fax: 41563334
E-mail: info@essessreference.com
www.essessreference.com

Cover Design by *Patch Creative Unit*

Printed and bound in India.

Dedicated to
My beloved Parents
LATE SRI S. VENKATRAMAN
and
SMT. GNANAMBAL VENKATRAMAN

Contents

Acknowledgements

We wish to express our sincere thanks and deep sense of gratitude to Ess Ess Publications, New Delhi for undertaking the publication of this book and their professional help in bringing out this volume. We sincerely thank IGM Library, University of Hyderabad for giving us an opportunity to work in an automated environment. We record our special thanks and gratitude to Prof S. Sudharshan Rao. Retd. Emeritus Professor, Osmania University Hyderabad, for his encouragement and coming forward to write the foreword. Finally we express our thanks to Dr N. Varatharajan, University Librarian, University of Hyderabad for his support.

V. Uma
V. J. Suseela

Preface

Library Automation though not a recent concept, it is evergreen as all the libraries in the developing countries are in the process of automating in-house operations irrespective of their type and size. Library automation is considered as advantageous in standardizing bibliographic records and relieving libraries from the tedious as well as repetitive processes. Until recently the automation was optional activity for libraries and limited to few larger libraries with fewer operations like cataloguing, circulation of books etc. The concept has been gaining prominence in recent times and drawing the attention of most of the practicing librarians and LIS schools in developing countries including India. Moreover, it is made mandatory by the government departments, quality assessment as well as accrediting agencies, who have been encouraging foundations/consortia to design and develop LIS software for the benefit of their member libraries. For example UGC INFLIBNET has developed SOUL software and supplying to university/college libraries at nominal costs while providing training facilities for automating their in-house operations. Many commercial as well as open source LIS software have already entered the field with varied processes, facilities and customizable options e.g. Libsys, Libris, Newgenlib, Koha, VTLS, e-grandhalaya, SOUL etc.

The objective of any library is primarily to serve the user community by providing right information to the right reader at right time with the latest technologies and tools. The father of library science and profession in India, Dr. S.R. Ranganathan described that the users, books and staff as the integral and inseparable components of library and thus called as "trinity of library".

Most of the public and academic libraries especially of colleges are yet not able to implement automation programs due to lack of funds and also expertise. These libraries are encountering with customization issues in case of commercial software as no software is sufficiently supporting all the library operations according to procedures followed by Indian libraries. Further, these libraries are also facing installation/ update problems with Open source software. Thus most of the software's whether commercial or open source are posing many practical issues and remain unresolved during implementation.

The book **"Automation of Library Integrated Operations : A How to do Manual"** deals with all the current aspects of automation and the issues that need to be addressed while implementing automation in their respective libraries. The Library automated systems those support in house operations, users as well as management information needs through conventional acquisition, cataloguing, Serials, circulation modules are dealt in detail illustrating the main processes and also the other supporting operations like article indexing, bindery, security, stock/stack maintenance management, audit and user information systems etc. The latest web applications viz. mobile, RFID technologies are discussed in the context of enhancing the effects of library automation.

The contents of the book with practical inputs are designed for practicing librarians for implementing automation in their libraries and the LIS students to learn the most significant aspects of the discipline as well as the profession. It will also be helpful for the librarians who have implemented automation programs also to launch new services with additional features and to rectify the errors occurred in manual process, because a professional librarian can understand the issues and corrections etc., but not the computer personnel who design the product. Hence, this book will be more useful for practising librarians and also software vendors to update software with additional features. Further, the Librarians can evaluate the software, based on the features mentioned in this book and select the software based on their library requirements. The covers the following chapters.

1. Library Automation: an Overview
2. Automation of Acquisition Processes
3. Automation of Cataloguing Processes
4. Automation of Circulation Operations
5. Automation of Serials Control and Holdings
6. Library Integrated Management Systems : An Overview of Various software
7. User Interface, The Web OPAC
8. Automation of Library Maintenance Services
9. Conclusion

Chapter 1. Library Automation an overview : This chapter gives an understanding of library automation prerequisites, evolution of automation, principles of automation, Infrastructure facilities like user environment (LAN), network components, hardware components like client server architecture, server, console, switches, Hubs and Fibre optic cable and hardware components of modern security systems like electronic security gates and RFID (Radio Frequency Identification) and the benefits of automation.

Chapter II. Automation of Acquisition Processes explains the functions that are required in automation similar to manual function from duplicate checking of books, ordering the books to the final payment by providing fund transfer from one budget to another and handling acquisition processes of different type of library materials either by gift or exchange. Feasibility of Currency exchange rates, flow chart of acquisition processes and to minimize data entry. The possibility of merging acquisition records with cataloguing when the full details of the book is received. Sharing of acquisition data across all other subsystems. Showing the exact status of the book in OPAC i-e online in process data.

Chapter III. Deals with Automation of Cataloguing processes. In this the standards to be followed such as MARC 21 and AACR2 is emphasized. It stresses the importance of shared cataloguing thereby duplicaticn of intellectual effort in the cataloguing the same resource can be avoided. By automating the cataloguing function the professional intelligence can be used for other services. Following the standards the catalogue records can be shared internationally, nationally and regionally. This brings about uniformity, consistency and completeness of the catalogue record. The standards of Z39.50 protocol and ISO-2709 help in interoperability and exchange of records in a networking environment. This chapter gives in a nutshell the features required in the cataloguing module. The problems encountered during automation and ways of correcting the bibliographic record is mentioned. MARC21 fields and the tags for cataloguing electronic resources are also highlighted. The importance of cataloguing module as a central database which can be shared across other modules is indicated.

Chapter IV. Automation of Circulation Operations gives a view of circulations transactions like Issue and return of books, creating patron record with membership privileges. Borrower's history, over dues, fine collection etc with reminder functions are mentioned. Online renewal of books and reservation of books are also dealt. Compatibility of circulation operations with barcode technology and other security systems is covered. Transactions log can be viewed to know the book that are highly in demand and order additional copies of the same book. Borrowing a book from one library and returning it from other branch library is made possible in automation of circulation operations. The users can view the borrowing details by registering and logging into through web OPAC. The automation of circulation operations highly are user centric and the users can easily borrow the book and also view the transactions while borrowing or returning in a double screen with a connecting device or adopter.

Chapter V. Automation of Serial Control and Holdings deal with subscription management, registering issue sending reminders etc. The Complicated issue related to publication of serials like delayed publication out of turn issues, change of title and renewal of previous year titles for the current are the issues that need to be addressed by most of the software vendors. From acquisition module the titles of serials are taken for renewing the serials which is problematic. Binding the loose issues and ordering the same with the binders by displaying the status of the item on the OPAC are mentioned. The serials subscription and receiving the issues with automatically scheduling the expected issues are covered with flow chart.

Chapter VI. Discusses about six Integrated Library Management System Software such as Koha, New Gen Lib Open source software and Commercial software like Libsys, Visionary Technlogy for Library solutions (VTLS), SOUL and e-Granthalaya a software mainly designed to meet the requirements of group libraries and Government Libraries. The modules in these software are discussed with comparisons. The screen shot of modules in each software are provided which will help libraries to have an Understanding of these software while going in for automation of all the operations in the library. They can know the features of these software and also the functions that are required during automation of their library collection.

Chapter VII. Gives an idea of user interface, Web OPAC. The basic characteristics of OPAC. The basic search, advanced search and Boolean operators like AND or NOT are explained. The different generations of OPAC are narrated. Users can query through OPAC for recommending a book is mentioned. The expectations of the users in the ever changing technology environment is also discussed. The mobile applications of web OPAC as a modern user tool is stated. The future Web OPACS using Google interface will be able to provide much more functionalities.

Chapter VIII. Library Maintenance in Automation Environment gives in a nutshell that several registers can be generated through Library integrated operations. Primarily the acquisition operations.

Maintenance functions like Stack maintenance and updating the status of book in the system is important to provide the correct and exact information to the user. The Stock verification report generation is mentioned in an automated environment. Maintenance system enables to manage the status of library material and also be able to modify the status of an item from available to missing or in-bindery or even turn to non-circulatory etc. Integration of web 2.0 technologies such as Blogs, Wikis, Podcasts, and RSS feeds, instant messaging, social networking etc. to library web OPACs have made OPACs more user centric and enable users to interact with the library. The sharing of user's feedback or opinions through web 2.0 tools integration to library web OPAC is very useful.

Chapter IX. It is a concluding chapter giving some suggestions in an automated environment. Proper manual and documentation is necessary in any automated environment. Depending up on the collection and fund position one has to choose the software suitable for their library. Manual should be available online and the details of the software should be referred at the time of entering whenever doubt arises. At the time of installation testing should be done. All the modules functionality should conform to the manual operations. Resource Description Access (RDA) the modern standard in cataloguing as a successor of AACRII is mentioned.

V. Uma
V.J. Suseela

Prof. S. Sudarshan Rao
UGC Emeritus Fellow
Formerly: ICSSR Senior Fellow

Department of Library an Information Science
OSMANIA UNIVERSITY
HYDERABAD - 500 007.
Email: [illegible]
Mobile: [illegible]

FOREWORD

I am extremely delighted to find a manual on library automation entitled *Automation of Library Integrated Operations,* authored by Dr V Uma and Dr V J Suseela, the two Deputy Librarians of IGM Library, University of Hyderabad. IGM Library is considered as the premier university library in India to automate all the library operations and to undertake turnkey operations to help in automation of other libraries.

It's a long time desire and a felt need for a working manual, as a helping tool in aid of the professional librarians of all types of libraries, especially for benefit of the younger generation of professionals and also the students of LIS programmes. The present manual is expected to fulfil such a desire. Further, it is construed that this work is the result of the authors' rich professional experience of more than three decades in a reputed automated library and digital library, the IGM library.

Over the last few decades, the libraries underwent lot many transformations, transcending from traditional libraries to the automated libraries and eventually to the digital or virtual libraries. In this process, Automation of libraries is an essential and transitory phase of shifting from traditional to automated libraries, and moving further on to the digital libraries. Computers and communication technologies, viz., ICTs (Information and Communication Technologies) have brought in tremendous transformation in almost all the library operations, techniques and services in terms of creation and publishing documents, especially the c-resources and web resources; recording and creating of inventories of documents; searching and retrieval of information / documents; sharing and dissemination / delivery of information, etc in an easy and timely manner.

Twenty first century is witnessing a peculiar situation of information abundance or information overflow. This is felt not just because of growth of print resources, but because of the proliferation of information and its availability in variant forms, such as, e-books, c-journals, web resources, bibliographic & full text databases, open access resources, resources offered through consortia, etc. The challenge before the present day libraries and librarians is on how to manage with the ever increasing information overload and how to identify, tap and deliver the relevant information to the information seekers / users in a timely manner and of course, with precision. Fulfilling the two important fundamental laws of Library Science, viz., 'Books / Information is for use', and 'Save the time of Users' has become a really difficult task for the present day librarians and information managers. Automation of libraries, switching on to digital libraries and making use of the ICTs and web technologies are found to be the solutions in this direction.

Automation of libraries, though began in 1970s with standalone modules transformed into an integrated system of all the modules / operations and subsequently with the advent of ICTs and web technologies it has become more a user centric system where, a user can log in to the library OP AC and find the books of interest and can ask for the issue of the books) or other documents of his / her interest. In the changed context, the library automation is basically meant for unfolding the library resources to its readers and to deliver the services at a quicker pace.

The focus of the present manual is on various aspects of library automation, such as Infrastructure requirement for Library Automation - the hardware and software, automation process of acquisitions, automated cataloguing and OPACs, Circulation, Serials Control, records maintenance and management. It also presents a comparative account of the features and facilities available with various integrated library software systems, both proprietary and open source such as, Libsys, VTLS, e-Granthalaya, SOUL, NewGenLib, and KOHA to facilitate librarians in selecting suitable software for their libraries, depending on their requirements.

The publication is found to be a valuable tool to the budding professionals and the students of LIS programmes, besides others in the LIS profession. It covers almost all the issues and problems involved in the process of automation of libraries. Serials control and management issues such as, generation of ad-hoc reports, renewals of serials in to the current years, changing the vendors, etc are well covered in this work. However, such features are missing in many of the integrated library software. The book also covers various other current developments and new features of library automation such as, mobile apps for viewing Web OPACs. Finally, it can be well said that it is a useful addition to the exiting literature in the field of Library and Information Science and a dependable tool that helps in solving the problems of automation and a guiding tool.

S Sudarshan Rao

List of Tables

List of Figures

List of Abbreviations

ISSN	International standard serial number
URL	Uniform resource locator
CD-ROM	Compact disc read only memory
RAM	Random access memory
E-RAMS	Electronic resource management service
NISO	National information standards organization
NCIP	Circulation and interchange protocol
XML	Extensible Markup Language
MS-SQL	Microsoft Structured Query Language
API	Application program interface
ILMS	Integrated library management systems
HTML	Hypertext markup language
PPF	Portable document format
NDT	Visual display terminal
TCP\IP	Transmission control protocol/Internet protocol
EDT	Electronic data transmission
LORLS	Loughborough online reading list system
OCLC	Online Computer Library Centre
LOC	Library of Congress
DELNET	Developing Library Network
INFLIBNET	Information Library and Network

ISBD	International Standard Bibliographic Description
AACR	Anglo American Cataloguing Rules
CCF	Common Communication Format
UNIMARC	Universal Marc Format
DCMI	Dublin Code Metadata Initiative
RDF	Resource Description Framework
RDA	Resource Description Access
Retro conversion	Retrospective conversion
CDS\ISIS	Computerized Documentation system \ Integrated set for Information Systems
ILL	Inter Library Loan
MEDLARS	Medical Literature Analysis and Retrieval System
KWIC	Keyword in context
KWOC	Keyword out of context
SDI	Selective Dissemination of Information
CAS	Current Awareness Service
OCR	Optical Character Recognition
LAN	Local Area Network
DBMS	Database Management System
AIDC	Auto Identification Data Collection
RFID	Radio Frequency Identification
EM	Electromagnetic
EAS	Electronic Article Surveillance
OS	Operating System
RDBMS	Relational Database Management System
COM	Computer Output Microfiche
INSDOC	Indian National Scientific Documentation Centre

DESIDOC	Defence Scientific Information & Documentation Centre
NISSAT	National Information System for Science and Technology
UNESCO	United Nations Educational, Scientific and Cultural Organization

1

Library Automation : An Overview

1.1. INTRODUCTION

Library automation is not a recent concept, new technologies that evolve over the period, compel the libraries for the dynamic implementation of in-house operations that enhance the accessibility of products and user services time to time. Libraries mainly deal with large number of bibliographic records. Some standards and standardization of processes are required for maintaining of databases, as the uniformity and consistency are the prime keys to achieve accuracy at all stages. For perfect automation, libraries need to adhere to international standards and networks for exchanging and sharing the bibliographic database to avoid duplication of work. Librarians need to handle computer with application software, computing skills with sound knowledge of library functionalities to create and maintain bibliographic databases. Librarians need to be aware of software technologies used for client server architecture, search engines and web based applications.

1.2. EVOLUTION OF AUTOMATION

The early efforts of library automation are traced during 1950s by using several semi- automated methods; those were later evolved with the use of digital computers. These semi-automated methods were superseded by computer-based systems, as they were less prone to errors, increasing speedy operations and further evolved to be able to integrate in-house operations accessing internal as well as external resources and share the local resources form into global resources. In each phase of evolution of library automation, there has been a greater influence of technological advancements in the physical format of information, dissemination medium, communication networks, and database management systems. In broad sense, the library automation since 50s has evolved through 3 incremental phases – efficiency of internal operations, accessing local resources and external resources. Thus it is described as a shift from local concerns to global concerns (Haravu, 2004)

These factors are directing libraries in delivering the best services to users. Library Automation began with information retrieval. Machine searching of bibliographic records started with MEDLARS (Medical Literature Analysis and Retrieval System) and was operational in 1964. It concentrated on two products. The composition of Index, Medicus enabled searching of large files of journal article citations for production of bibliographies and for on demand search output. This was the pioneering attempt to make big bibliographic databases on computers, which served as a model for other database vendors for providing bibliographic database online systems for remote access. This also provided Boolean 'AND', 'OR', 'NOT' operators in searching.

Later H.P Luhn in 1961 used it for KWIC (keyword in context) which served as index to the titles of articles in chemical abstracts. KWIC used words in the title and listed alphabetically, while KWOC (Keyword out of context) provided words listed separately. KWIC & KWOC provided multiple access to documents listed in current awareness publication. He also proposed the idea of SDI (selective dissemination of information (SDI) service using user profiles and matching document profiles based on the interests of the users in libraries and information centres. Even today, such services are found and called as "push" services provided by web portals.

The British Library started automation (Coward, 1977 & Butcher 1993) by converting catalogue records using keypunching which was followed by using optical character recognition (OCR) which was an advanced technology at that time. Efforts were made to create National Bibliographic System. At the Lending Division, Elsevier initiated trials with ADONIS a system for digitising images of articles for transmission to users. It was superseded by similar superior systems that are now in general use.

1.3. PRINCIPLES OF LIBRARY AUTOMATION

The three principles of system selection throughout the migration process can help to assure a successful outcome. They are –

1. Concentrating on the organization's context
2. Secondly by choosing long-term over short-term benefits, and
3. Finally by involving staff and users throughout the process

An organization that is automating or changing systems must review time-honoured practices in order to determine if they remain cost-effective. They must be the practices that best help the patrons during the change of environment.

The data in the system should represent greater Investment than the software through which you access it. It may be tempting to minimize the pain of the normal chaotic transition by adapting to shortcuts as well compromising with the normal quality standards for cataloguing, acquisitions, serials check-in or other processes. Such compromises are not in the best interest of the organization, even if they greatly reduce the stress of the system migration. Therefore, the choice of infrastructure is very essential for the successful implementation of automation in libraries.

1.4. LIBRARY AUTOMATION - INFRASTRUCTURE

1.4.1. User Environment

In an integrated system, staff and patrons have access to the information at one place. Integrated system helps library patrons to view the bibliographic record and also know the status of the book whether it is checked out and at the same time protecting the borrower‘s personal details by restricting the display on OPAC screen. However, users can login to their own account and also know the acquisition status of book. The end user thus become familiar with the operations are also a full partner in the implementation process of automation.

Through internet and technology, the integrated system has transformed from mere sharing bibliographic record among other modules to a system that allows to exchange information with other systems outside the library system. The library can order the book by drawing information from publishers' website. Through OPAC patrons can also view other bibliographic databases of both inside and outside the home library. Today's web based integrated systems are built on client server architecture and the client server architecture allows standardization protocols for transmitting information within and outside the organization.

1.4.2. Network Scenario

Library automation can be implemented in different networked environments. In distributed network of libraries, the main library with branch or department libraries can share the same software and be part of the main library with different sub-locations. Different public libraries or academic libraries may exist using different library software's but can share their resources through resource sharing networks or consortia. This also comes under distributed network of libraries.

In a hierarchical network, the main library will undertakes all the processing and only minimal tasks like issues & returns will be handled by the departmental library sharing the same software.

Single User Environment

In a single user environment the staff user has a visual display terminal connected to a personal computer which has a hard disk drive on which the application programs and databases are loaded. The same PC will be used for updating database and to retrieve information by the users for any purpose.

There can be a CD drive and printer connected to the PC. The staff user can add records to the database; search the catalogue and produce printed catalogue cards also. This type of system is called single user system.

Multi user system

In this type many users will access the computer system which has library automation application software and data files. The complexities are handled by a special piece of hardware called the terminal server to manage the sending and receiving of the data between the central processing unit and user terminal. When a particular user sends the message to the host computer it is routed through the terminal server which corrects any errors and sends back the data to the central processor. This helps in preventing two or more users updating the same record simultaneously. In such a situation the other user who tries to open the same record is prevented by popping up alert message that 'the record is closed for updating'.

Local Area Networks (LAN)

This local area networks functions at a faster rate than telephone lines but the distances are limited and there is also a limit on the number of computers that can be connected to a single LAN. This is possible because of the standard networking protocols and media. Many business houses, educational organizations and libraries use this type of network. Each node or workstation in a LAN has its own CPU with which it executes programs and also be able to access data and devices anywhere on the LAN. The users in LAN can share data as well as expensive laser printers. They can communicate with email and chat facilities. In a network there is a server that stores data files and delivers data and programs to user work stations. The LAN is built using coaxial or fibre optic or twisted pair cables. Each PC on LAN will be connected via network adaptor cord or internet cord. LANs are based on the file sharing architectures where the servers download files from the shared location to the desktop environment.

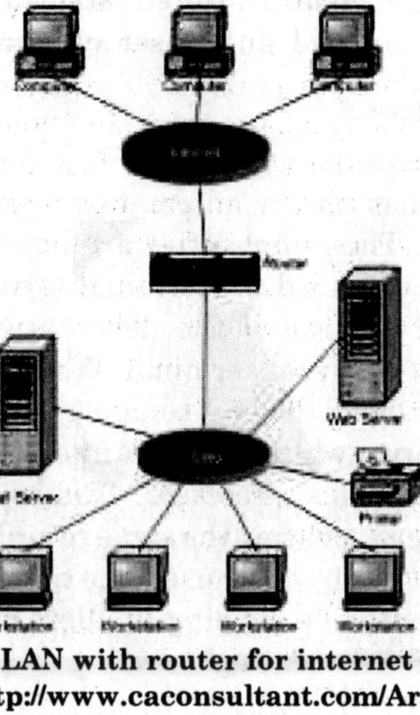

Fig. 1.1. LAN with router for internet access
(*Source* : http://www.caconsultant.com/Article/VPN/introduction_to_vpn.htm)

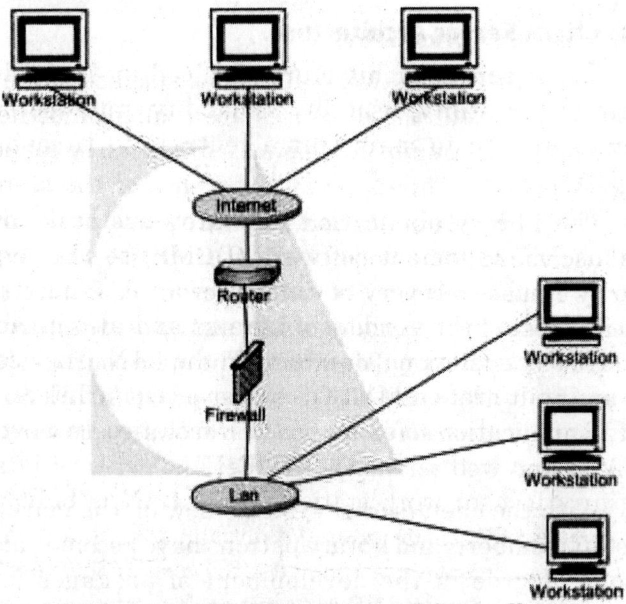

Fig. 1.2. LAN with router and firewall to control external access (*Source* : http://www.caconsultant.com/Article/VPN/introduction_to_vpn.htm)

The application software resides on the server and used by the users at the different terminals. The programs are then executed on user workstations. The system administrator manages permissions through DBMS to add, modify, edit and delete records in the databases. PC based LANs required network operating system software enhances a basic operating system by adding networking features. The disadvantage of LAN system led to the evolution of client server architecture in libraries.

1.5. HARDWARE SPECIFICATIONS

When we talk about automation it is also necessary that we need to understand certain computer hardware components that are required for working with automation software in a networking environment.

1.5.1. Client Server Architecture

Client server architectures evolved in 1980s due to improved versatility, usability scalability, interoperability when compared to main frame centralized timesharing computers.

The library application software's are built around database management software (DBMS) to take care of security issues, recovery of data in event of failure of the system. Most of the vendors of LIS software structure their catalogue as a relational database. The open source software also are built around MY-SQL server or ORACLE. Some of the LIS application software use web browser software, such as JAVA and web server i.e. APACHE.

With the client/server systems now on the market, all the staff members, and library patrons have become partners to some degree in the development of packages for the automation process.

In 1990's as everyone started using internet, security problem has become a big concern and hence firewalls were installed to meet the purpose.

1.5.2. Server & Console

According to Wikipedia in computing server is defined, "a server is a computer program or a device that provides functionality for other programs or devices, called "clients". This architecture is called the client–server model, and a single overall computation is distributed across multiple processes or devices. Servers can provide various functionalities, often called "services", such as sharing data or resources among multiple clients, or performing computation for a client. A single server can serve multiple clients, and a single client can use multiple servers. A client process may run on the same device or may connect over a network to a server on a different device. Typical servers are database servers, file servers, mail servers, print servers, web servers, game servers, and application servers.

Server is referred as a computer program providing services to other computer programs and their users in the same or other computers. A computer, in which a server program runs in, is also a server even if it is used for other purposes also. In the client/server programming the server is a program which waits and responds to the requests from client programs in the same or other computers. Sometimes it will function as a client in a given application with requests for services from other programs and also function as a server of requests from other programs.

Console

Console server is a software that can be run on a UNIX box with number of serial ports. When we plug consoles of other machines into the serial ports, it permits us to access these consoles on the network from anywhere. Console servers and terminal servers both provide a number of serial ports which are then connected to the serial ports of other equipment.

1.5.3. Routers, Switches, Hub & Optical Cable etc.

Router

Router is used for forwarding data packets along networks. A minimum of two networks are needed for a router to connect usually two LANs or WANs and its ISPs network. Wherever two or more networks are connected routers are placed at gateways. Headers and forwarding tables are used by routers to determine the best way for forwarding the packets. Routers use Internet Control Message Protocol (ICMP) to communicate and configure the best path between any two hosts. ICMP is an error reporting protocol and it is a further extension of Internet Protocol.

Switch

Switch is used for filtering and forwarding packets between LAN segments thereby, operating at the data link layer or else the network layer of the OSI Reference Model and support any packet protocol. When switches are used to join segments it is switched LANs and similarly in Ethernet networks they are called as switched Ethernet LANs.

Hub

Hub is a common connecting point for devices in a network. For connecting segments of a LAN hubs are used which contains multiple ports. To make all segments of the LAN to view all the packets, a packet when arrived at one port is copied to other ports.

Fibre Optical Cable

In this glass (or plastic) threads (fibers) are used to transmit data. A fiber optic cable consists of a bundle of glass threads, each of which is capable of transmitting messages modulated onto light waves. Fiber optic cable is a data transmission medium with high-speed .It contains tiny glass or plastic filaments that carry light beams. Through the *cable* via rapid pulses of light digital data is transmitted.

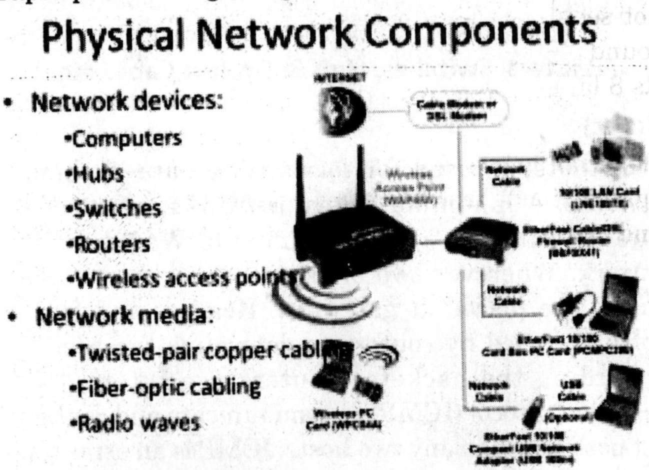

Fig. 1.3. Network Components

1.5.4. Modern Integrated Security System in Libraries

Along with automation of in house library operations it is necessary to safe guard the materials from theft and to make it more user prone by facilitating quick borrowing it is pertinent to know the latest electronic gates to arrest theft. Depending up on the libraries budget, financial capacity and collection a library can install electronic security gates.

The hardware requirements for the security of library materials and easy functioning of library patron operations we need to install electronic security gates. Along with automation of inhouse operations to offer quick and better services to the users it is necessary to install electronic security systems which works with ILS and has seamless integration with the Integrated Library system offering user prone services. Some of them are described here under with the illustrations

3M electromagnetic security gate, Ellipse 2020

3M security gate with electromagnetic identification tag uses electromagnetic technology to arrest theft. Electromagnetic strips are pasted into the books which are not seen but identified at the security gate with the beep sound if taken through unauthorized means. It costs around Rs 8 lakhs.

Barcode and security labels/strips – use of three types of permanently, sensitized labels and strips for security against theft, tracking of materials throughout processing and circulation

Fig. 1.4. 3M Security Gate for Libraries

AIDC (Automatic Identification Data Collection) technology is of both barcode-based data collection and wireless communication system with equipment, pre-packaged and fully customized solutions for every aspects of data management.

Ellipse 2020 library security system (Dialoc ID-Netherlands) is a method for protection of all library materials such as books, CD's Audio cassettes and microfiche. It makes use of Electromagnetic technology with diagnostic signal rating and switch capacitor filtering to provide better efficiency. Visible and audio alarms alert the library staff during theft of library material. It costs around 10 lakhs.

Radio-frequency identification (RFID)

RFID Security system, is a modern security system with integrated features which generally uses electromagnetic (EM) or Radio Frequency Technology to control theft and also for other library operations like Inventory control, re shelving, searching of library materials

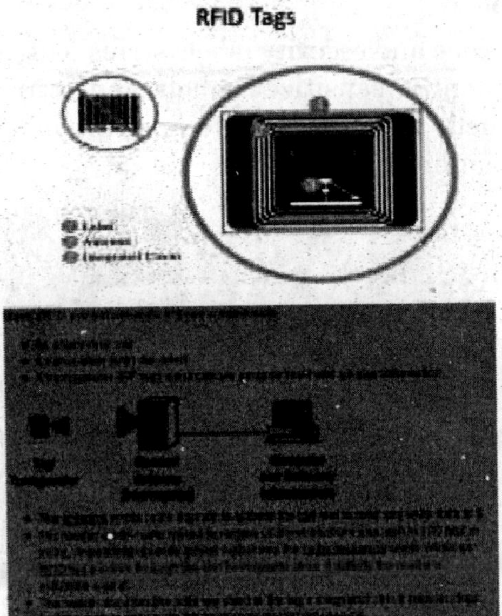

Fig. 1.5. Components of RFID

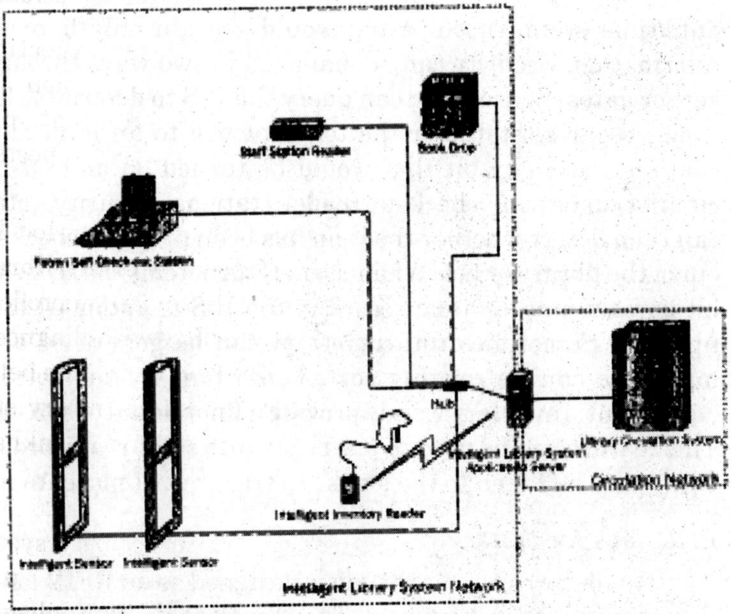

Source: Checkpoint Systems.

Fig. 1.6. RFID enabled library environment

The Traditional barcode is replaced with an RFID tag and the barcode scanner is swapped for an RFID reader:

The Functions are

- Helps Self-check out
- Saves the time in, check in and re shelving of returned books
- Locating of missing items in the stacks with ease and speed
- Users are provided with better quality services by ensuring that new library items reach the shelves sooner.

RFID tag is programmed with unique information about the item which can be imported from (ILS) an integrated library system at the tag programming station. Information about different types of material can be included on the tag (such as book title, Patron circulation information, date/time stamps), but a tag would contain only barcode information. Security can be managed in two ways through sensor gates. Sensor gate can query the ILS to determine an item's security status or the tag attached to an item may contain a security bit that would be turned on and off by circulation or self –checkout reader stations. Security gates can then detect whether the item has been properly checked out of the library or not. When users return items the security bit is reset and the item record in the ILS is automatically updated. Sometimes return receipt can be generated and materials can be roughly sorted into bins by the return equipment. Inventory wands provide a finer detail of sorting. This feature can be used to put books into shelf-ready order. It can also be taken to the stacks to trace out of place items.

RFID Tags for Library

In library systems the tag is designed as an RFID label that consists of four elements. They are the chip, the antenna on the foil, the cover or plastic label and the silicon liner. Passive tags are used for library application, which draw electric power through an inductive field generated by a reader. Passive tags are smaller in size, cheaper and are long lasting than active tags. Passive tags do not broadcast the information stored on the tag unless they are requested by a reader.

RFID reader for Library

The reader generates the electrical impulse that causes the tag to be read because the tags used in libraries are usually passive. The reader interrogates the tag then the tag answers with the information stored on the tag. Some readers store the information captured from the tags while others capture the information and immediately pass it through to the database or ILS. The readers are configured to identify tags for the purpose of circulation which also serves as inventory management and theft control. Readers are either fixed or handheld and are located in the library.

Tagging station is used to program the tags to be attached to the library materials

- Staff workstation at circulation is used to charge and discharge library materials
- Self-check station is used to check-in and checkout library materials without staff assistance
- Book-drop station is used to automatically discharge library materials and reactivate security
- Sorter and conveyor automated system for returning material to proper area of library
- Sensor gates are used to verify that all material leaving the library has been checked out
- Inventory manager is used for inventorying and verifying that material is shelved correctly

Features

- Helps to Detect EAS (Electronic Article Surveillance)
- Multi item detectable to integrate camera with the gate
- Feasibility to integrate with surveillance gate

Advantages

- This technology serves double purpose both inventory and theft management
- The beep sound alerts Library staff immediately when unauthorized item is passing through.
- Would be thieves are alerted immediately and are deterred with the physical presence at the gate.
- The camera on the gate captures numbers of users passing through the gate
- Alarmed volume can be easily controlled.

Counter station

Counter staff is provided with series of functions such as loan return, tagging and sorting etc. It is loaded with alarming /disarming module and sorting module. This EAS bit inside the library material is set/reset so as to trigger/ not to trigger alarm on the gate.

Features

a. Editing and updating of user record

b. Adding and deleting of user record

c. Generate loan history for a particular user

d. Managing the funds incurred by users

e. Program of adding a new library material

f. Sort items according to their branch and category number

Check-in & check-out station

The user check in and check out station is basically a computer with touch screen and a built in RFID Reader plus special software for personal identification ,books and other library material handled at the circulation. This is done with personal identification of the user ID number, a barcode/ personal ID number (PIN). The user is asked to choose the next action, checkout of one or several items. It is also possible for check in transactions.

Book drop station

This can be located anywhere in the school/shopping Centre/Railway station. Material can be returned any time. Users insert the library item into the slot. The Reader captures the electronic signature and sends to back end system for loan cancellation. The user is acknowledged by beep sound and flashlight thereby the user record is updated immediately. This is possible due to the seamless link between the RFID management system and the host computer system. The users can start borrowing items once they have returned the books through book drop.

Shelf Management System

It is a portable scanner and a base station locating and identifying items on the shelves.

a. It helps to search for individual book that is returned

b. Inventory check of the whole library stock

c. Search for the book that is misplaced /not properly shelved.

All these functions are performed by swiping the shelves to gather their identities. In an inventory check situation the identities collected are compared with the book databases and a discrepancy report is generated.

Advantages

a. No more book handling

b. Just passing of the reader across shelved books to perform an instant inventory

c. Accuracy; Book identification makers are registered in the shelf management Reader. The data is then downloaded to the central database

d. Quick Inventory check: 20 books per second.

e. Notification: Books to be pulled are uploaded to the reader for quick identification

f. Quick and correct shelving of items that raise the efficiency of shelf arrangement.

Server/Docking station

This is the communication gateway among various components. It is a station in which the software that interfaces with the automated library system is loaded. The software includes Application Programming Interfaces. It receives the information from one or more readers and exchanges information with the circulation database. The server includes a transaction database so that reports can be produced.

Benefits of RFID

Benefits to library management

- Improved security within the library

- Efficient collection management system
- Improved collection security
- Flexible staff schedules
- Labor saving methods free the staff to help customers
- Higher customer patron satisfaction levels
- Improved inter-library cooperation
- Better preservation of inventory because of less handling by staff
- Same security and labeling formats for all items such as books, CDs & DVDs and hence better management of databases.

Benefits for library staff

- Time saving methods that free the staff and thereby help customers better
- Labor saving methods free them from doing same repetitive jobs and stressful tasks.
- Flexible work schedules are possible.

Benefits for library patron

- Faster check in & check out for all types of items(Books, CDs, DVDs, audio &video tapes etc)
- More staff available for service
- Quicker user service such as payment of fees ,fines etc
- Better inter library loan facilities and efficient reservation facilities
- Faster and accurate re-shelving thus patrons can find items in their place and better satisfying service.

RFID disadvantages

- RFID is costly. If a funding agency can come forward the library can use the latest technology.
- It is possible to disrupt the function of RFID system by wrapping the protected material in two to three layers of ordinary foil to block the radio signal

- The RFID technique can be fooled by placing two items against one another so that one tag overlays another. This requires technology knowledge and careful alignment.
- While the short range readers used for check out/check in and inventorying appear to read the tags accurately most of the time the performance of the exit gate sensors is not so good.
- The signal from one reader can interfere with the signal from another in the same coverage and affect the read accuracy.

The security system used in the library should be user friendly to achieve efficiency in handling members record and details, reduces error in circulation, unique in identifying the location and status of various tools like books, journals, standard periodicals, abstracts, audio and video cassettes etc. Electronic Article Surveillance (EAS) technology helps the library to identify items as they pass through a gated area, which alerts the unauthorized removal of items from the library. By placing EAS tags in the books, the chances of theft can be controlled. The Electronic security gate is to arrest the pilferage of books and unauthorized movement of books through the security gate with a beep sound to alert library staff of the not issued out book is being taken out through the gate. Electromagnetic full circulation Check out and Check in equipment should be used to issue the books to the readers. Full circulation entails Turning off the security strip (deactivation) and on (reactivation) at the circulation desk. ID system security books processing equipment is designed to help streamline check-out/check-in procedure.

1.6. SOFTWARE SPECIFICATIONS

Software specifications lays the foundation for library operations and we need to know some of the software's like server software ,operating system, application software to work with automation.

1.6.1. Server Software

According of techopedia "Server software is a type of software that is designed to be used, operated and managed on a computing server. It provides and facilitates the harnessing of underlying server computing power for use with an array of high-end computing services and functions". Server software is primarily designed to mainly interact with a server's hardware infrastructure, which includes the processor, memory, storage, input/output (I/O) and other communication ports. There are various types of server software like Web server software, Application server software, Database server software, Cloud computing server software and File server software. These server software uses the server for various functions and services focusing on inherent computer capacity and resources.

1.6.2. Operating system (OS)

The operating system is system software that manages all the hardware and software components thereby providing common services for computer programs. It is most important program that runs on a computer. Operating systems tasks are to recognize input from the keyboard, to send output to monitor display screen, to take care of files and directories on the disk, and to control peripheral devices like disk drives and printers. Every computer should have an operating system to run other programs and applications.

1.6.3. Relational Database Management System (RDBMS)

Open source library integrated software like KOHA and NewGenLib use My SQL and Postgres for backup recovery and indexing features. ORACLE, the RDBMS is used for VTLS the international commercial LIS software. Library databases are built around DBMS. If it is built around advanced RDBMS, it will take care of data organization, data security, recovery of data in the event of failure, data access across modules of ILS and information retrieval simultaneously by number of users. The relational

DBMS was developed during the 1970s and came to prominence during the 1980s and 1990s and so on. The initial DBMSs were hierarchical and network-based systems as per their structure and retrieval capability. The companies responded to the development of relational DBMSs and continued to focus on RDBMS products applications of query oriented usages and transaction-processing applications. It facilitated reduction in data redundancy, enabled to retrieve multiple logical files from the same data. 1980s was very important in the evolution of database systems as the relation model developed by E.F. Codd and others in 70s became widespread and achieved commercial acceptance.

Relational tables follow certain conditions to ensure the accuracy and accessibility of the data.

1.6.4. Application Software

Application software's are computer programs designed to suit end user needs. They include database programs, word processor, web browsers and spread sheet etc. Application software is loaded over the system software as it cannot be run without system software. An application can manipulate text, numbers, graphics, or a combination of these elements. Application software can be Educational software, Enterprise software, simulation software, Banking software, Entertainment software and Library application software.

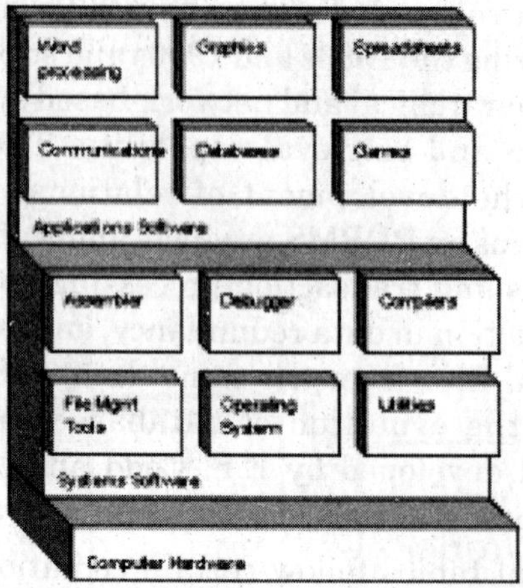

Fig. 1.7. Structure of Library System
http://www.webopedia.com/TERM/O/operating_system.html

1.7. LIBRARY HOUSE-KEEPING OPERATIONS

The machine readable cataloguing format (MARC) was initiated in 1961 comprising of tags with consisting of three digit numbers to represent personal name, title etc. The MARC format could not fulfil the standard bibliographic descriptions based on the AACR2 cataloguing code. So in 1968 the MARC2 project was initiated. The British National Bibliography and Library of Congress worked together towards UK MARC pilot project and LC MARC project in 1969 so that international exchange of records between USA and UK was possible. As many countries had their formats, the IFLA group worked on a common format UNIMARC in 1973, so that all the countries can exchange their bibliographic records. It was discussed in Paris in 1975 and in Brussels 1n1976 provisional version was available. The main aim was UNIMARC for content designation i.e. ISBD for all the data elements in the record. It was later on followed by OCLC for library automation and resource sharing. Many libraries began exchanging bibliographic records. The production of catalogue cards using computers was replaced with book form, and further by computer output microfiche

(COM). This could be easily distributed than book catalogues, but it was expensive, time consuming and difficult for consultation.

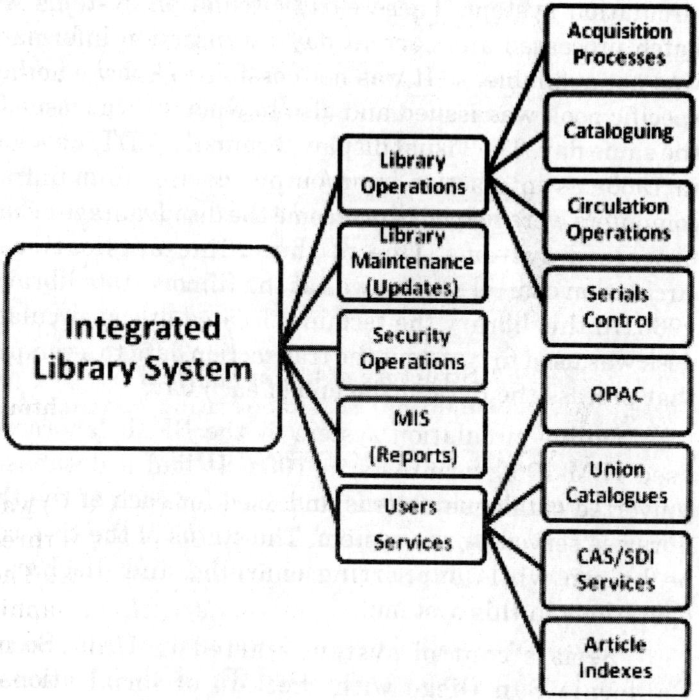

Fig. 1.8. Integrated Library System

The circulation control system used the punched card to store information about the books that were issued. It was tested in many university and public libraries in USA. This system produced loan lists, list of reserves as well as over dues for statistical analysis. In this system, book information was read from the punched card but borrower information was entered, whenever a charged transaction took place. A development in this area was the use of IBM-357 data collection device for circulation control by which it was feasible to have punched cards for both book card and borrower identification cards. The IBM-357 could read the punched cards and produce the paper tape of the transaction that was then fed to the computer programs in batch mode at the end of each day to generate outputs such as- lists of books on loan. The Southampton University library in UK was the first to use this application to automate the circulation system. These early circulation systems were batch processed and current day's transaction information was not available, so It was not possible to know whether a specific book was issued and also to whom it was issued on the same day. The visual display terminals (VDT) developed in 1960s as interactive input/output devices to mainframe computers were helped to overcome the disadvantage of batch processed systems. One of the online applications of circulation control system was at the Illinois state library in 1966. In this library the terminal located at the circulation desk was used to transmit the transaction data to a computer that process the data at the end of each day.

Online circulation system at the BELL laboratories used IBM-1050 terminals in 1968. It had a database of converted catalogue records and used for each of the three libraries served by the system. The status of the title could be known while supporting charging and discharging operations in this system.

Serials control system started in University of California San Diego with check-in of serial issues by retrieving manually the pre punched cards for each specific title and issue. The card was sent to computer centre for processing and the journal issue was sent to the shelves. By this system, subscription lists holding lists and list of issues not received could be generated. This was also used in Washington university school of medicine. The batch processed serials control system experienced many problems. The first online system at the Laval University in Quebec Canada was introduced by which file could be accessed from VDTs and the database could be searched and claims could be generated. Automation of acquisition system at the University of Michigan library was introduced with sophisticated system to produce multipart orders, in process lists and account statement of expenditure and encumbrances. The Washington State University library started the first online acquisition system in 1968 which could provide access by order number. The Stanford University libraries started online acquisition system in 1969. During 1970s to 80s due to technological development in computers, and the availability of commercial vendor software products librarians could share their experiences with the vendors. Earlier to this the University of Chicago library were one of the first users of MARC tapes distributed by the Library of Congress. The MARC tape was searchable by LC class number to identify new publications which was then ordered. The Stanford University developed the bibliographic automation of large library operations (BALLOTS) system which took care of the technical processing function of the Stanford University library. The four files of the BALLOT system consisted of a) MARC record for the previous six months; b) the in-process file; c) a catalogue data file containing a record for each item that was fully processed; and d) an authority file containing many see and see also references. Ballots had many search and retrieval facilities including the use of truncated terms, keywords and Library of Congress Subject Headings. This became the foundation for other libraries.

Online catalogues came into existence and became available on local area networks and through dialup modem connections by middle of 1980s. The online catalogues brought about many quality based improvements to access the library resources such as- search facility with keyword, Boolean logic and use of filters to limit the searches by publication year, language, form and type of material. To access the online resources outside the library, libraries began employing communication technologies. Consortia evolved policies for cooperative acquisitions, sharing of resources, skills and services and created a collective bargaining with vendor's, publishers and utilities such as OCLC. Important development for accessing the resources outside the library took place in 1980s and early 1990s resulting in automation and networking of libraries. The emergence of internet and the world wide web launched by Tim Burnes Lee in 1989 accelerated networking operations in automation of libraries. The breakthrough in internet history is the early 1980s is the development of transmission control protocol/ internet protocol (TCP/IP) by Vincent Cerf and his graduate students at the University of California at Los Angeles. This technology TCP/IP protocols allowed different computers to exchange data among themselves. Internet and www have great impact on the libraries. Because of the power of the microcomputer and internet, the information produced could be accessed from anywhere as long as it was hosted in the web server. The early use of internet has changed the roles and organizational culture of libraries and librarians since 1990. Integrated library software allowed access to circulation acquisition and cataloguing data and this transformed the very nature of the catalogue from a record of materials owned to a database to the extent indicating what owned is available or on order or borrowed by any of the registered users.

1.8. BENEFITS OF AUTOMATION

- Speed in processing the data
- Avoids redundancy and duplication of work
- Relieve the professional staff from the tedious processes of maintaining paper files for each operation, since the clients from other modules can retrieve data across the system. Tracking the status of records is easier.
- It is possible to assess staff output and performance with number of transactions executed in a day
- Maintain uniformity, consistency and standardization of processes to achieve the completeness of the records
- Maintaining authority control for bibliographic records
- Sharing the records and data across the modules thus minimizing repetition of data entry

- Showing the actual status of the record whether on order, received, on shelf or in binding.
- Receiving recommendations online and checking for duplication simultaneously informing to the concerned recommending authority regarding the acquisition status or availability of the book in the library.
- Using latest technologies for library functions such as mobile applications to access web OPAC etc.
- Main library can share not only records, but also the common procedures with the member libraries.
- Possible to convert currency rate by the system itself
- Electronic data transmission (EDT) enables transmitting recommendations, approvals, orders, notices, claims, payments etc. online.
- Users will be able to search and retrieve results quickly.
- Users will be able to view and maintain their account, renew books online, recommend for books, etc.

1.9. CONCLUSION

Hence, the libraries could automate their in-house operations in LAN environment and thereby OPAC could evolve as web OPAC enabling anyone to access or search records from anywhere.

While selecting the software the library should see whether the vendor's primary target aims at the type of libraries. Whether the product is with emerging trends in library field. Are they branded and have sufficient number of customers so that they will remain in the market for many years. Are they capable of attending to queries from the customers from time to time with enough resources? Do they have competent, knowledgeable persons to attend library problems? Do they release updated versions? Do they offer support for training and documentation? Feedback from other libraries using the software will further help to know the requirements and whether the requirements of library are met. The libraries can opt for stand-alone or integrated library system. Libraries can go for automating i.e. converting in the machine-readable form either one of the modules or all depending up on the size of the collection and budget. For automating, the library operations many softwares are available through commercial vendors (Libsys, VTLS) and also open source (Koha, NewGenlib and e-Grandalaya etc.).

An automated system is expected to be user friendly, increase the library's capacity in getting better status from different departments of the parent organization at the same time it should be simple to the users, and not requiring in depth understanding. The automated system should bring better status to the parent organization. In the beginning it should clearly reflect the success of using an automated system. It should be self-instructive and have tools like help and tutorials that help users to learn by themselves how to use it. The automation should prove to be successful in all the transactions pertaining to all the operations of the library. Less qualified staff with less qualifications and lower salaries than previously needed. It depends on well-organized planning procedures. A successful automation system will aim at increasing the quality of the library services without increasing the number of the staff. It should normally depend on the technical compatibility with other processes or modules in the library. The length of the time the vendor is in business should form the basis for the success of the system and requiring lesser training programs for the staff with ease of use. The automated system should be open for continued development and enhancement by providing good management information. The success of an automated system should have minimum downtime probably 1%. It should be compatible with the existing work procedures.

The following chapters will cover features, processes, automation requirements for each module in detail. Commercial & Open source software's are discussed to give an understanding about the functionalities of each module with regard to compatibility of software with library requirements, stack, stock, audit/finance and the maintenance procedures are also discussed.

The chapters of the book are designed in a way that facilitate both theoretical as well as a manual to direct the practising librarian how to do initiation, go with library automation processes and complexities and also learners in LIS schools. Library automation mainly aims to automate the in house operations such as :

- Library Automation : An Overview
- Automation of Acquisition Processes
- Automation of Cataloguing Processes
- Automation of Circulation Operations
- Automation of Serials Control and Holdings
- Library Integrated Management Systems- An Overview of Various Software
- User Interface, The Web OPAC
- Automation of Maintenance services
- Conclusion

2

Automation of Acquisition Processes

2.1. INTRODUCTION

The foremost function of acquisition module in library automation is to satisfy the information needs of its user community. The amount so allotted should be spent based on the purchase policies laid down by the parent organization. Libraries acquire different types of information material viz. in the form of books, serials, and non- book material such as CD-ROMs, microforms, video tapes etc. Earlier, the special libraries were giving importance to serials and less importance in the acquisition of books, whereas in the digital era the academic and public libraries, especially the university libraries give more importance to e-journals, e-books etc. through consortia/government initiatives. Apart from acquiring, the print material individual libraries have been spending lot of amount for the subscription of online journals and databases. Automation of acquisitions can help to reduce the tedious manual operations largely.

The automated acquisition system should be able to handle both technical and management i.e. bibliographic control, holdings management, order production and transmission, claims, recovery and accounting related problems. Management problems include cost control, collection development as well as management, resource allocation, personnel management and keeping track of budget and monitoring.

The latest development is at Loughborough University, learning and teaching has long been supported by the University Library's online reading list system. Students could access a web based view of their reading lists, and kept up to date in the academics by using their web browsers. Library staff made use of the reading list system to check whether important books are available in the library, for procuring additional copies based on the counts of student's access on each module.

Loughborough Online Reading List System (LORLS) is available as open sourced software under the GNU (an operating system -free software) General Public License version 2 and has been used at a number of different institutions. It can be downloaded from http://blog.lboro.ac.uk/lorls/downloads.

With the technological advancement applied in the book vendors 'online services it is possible to batch load bibliographic records for placing orders, either downloading records from the book vendor directly or loading through OCLC's PromptCat service.

2.2. NEED FOR AUTOMATION OF ACQUISITIONS

- It helps to relieve the staff members from maintaining several manual files, registers as, all the information entered can be retrieved either with author, title or order number, invoice number, voucher number etc.
- Once the data is entered can be recalled to update with necessary details such as edition number, price details etc. No data redundancy.
- Data is sharable across the other modules such as cataloguing and circulation

- Performance report of vendors can be generated to assess the best supplier for placing orders or renewal orders.
- Calculations of discount, postages and miscellaneous charges will be automatically done by the system and hence less prone to human errors.
- Users can login from OPAC to recommend/request the books or journals to be procured.
- The account status can be maintained from the stage of posting budgets to the respective accounts till the payment of invoice to vendors.
- Allocation of budget under different heads and balance amount can be automatically known once the order is placed under a particular account. Balance amounts automatically can be tracked to reallocate to another account, when there is a shortfall of funds in any account.
- Staff productivity and output can be generated to know the performance of the staff.
- Actual status of the book can be known such as on order, received or in-process, or on shelf etc.

2.3. BASIC FUNCTIONALITIES OF ACQUISITION SYSTEM

In addition to regular bibliographic data entry the library automation requires to handle acquisition processes such as receiving recommendations, approvals, orders, receipt of materials, invoices, payments and accounts etc. In automated acquisition system, some essential functionalities, controls, overrides, alerts etc are required to manage the system without errors. They are –

2.3.1. Control of Permissions

This type of control is required at record level and even field level. Some staff members are given data entry permissions while senior staff members are given permission to edit, modify and delete the records.

The users can only view the records but they cannot alter or change any record. Field level permission control includes the possibility of preventing the display of some data elements or unwanted information to users searching OPAC. In a network environment it is necessary to ensure that acquisition records are secured against loss due to system crashes or unauthorized access. The database administrator who also conducts audit trial of transactions usually does appropriate control and provision of permissions to different category of users. The underlying database management software, enable the database administrator to have proper control over transactions and recover the data in any event of failure.

2.3.2. Help Messages

It is highly essential to ensure that the system is tolerant to errors, which mean that while entering the data the users are likely to make mistakes. In such cases, the system should provide messages, which will help the users to correct the mistakes. For e.g. If all the processes of order is completed the message will appear as "order processed successfully". If the order number is a duplicate one the system prompts messages such as "order number already exists" which helps the staff to give a different order number. If the budget exceeds the amount for a particular year the system will prompt messages such as "the amount exceeds the budget limit". Such messages help the staff to work with the acquisition processes successfully and direct the staff to work minimizing the mistakes.

2.3.3. Data entry and update

Data entry is online, and interactive and user friendly. The data entry should be in the user friendly preformatted screens which enables the operator to enter the data sequentially one after another. For example author followed by title, subtitle etc. The records entered and its associated indexes should be immediately updated providing up-to-date information to staff/user clients. For example discount change entered should reflect in the fund account immediately. In a multiuser networking environment the system should support locking of records during updates so that number of persons cannot change or update the same record at a time as the message the record is being updated will appear if more than one person attempts to simultaneously change the same record.

When ISBN is entered it gets validated immediately. Most of the integrated automation systems help sharing data between files. Data from one or more files should be possible to be imported into acquisition records. For example, if a second copy of a book is required it should be possible to import the bibliographic data from online catalogue file into the acquisition records without additional data entry.

Data entry should be minimized as far as possible or eliminated for the logically linked files. While entering the data there should be possibility to define default values for various fields example date fields are automatically entered. To avoid data entry mistakes it is necessary to provide a pop up list of vendors while attempting to enter a new vendor. This avoids errors and promotes consistency.

Nowadays most of the operating systems support multitasking and permit more than one task at the same time. It helps to move from one task to another in the series of required tasks to be performed.

2.3.4. Over-riding Function

The system should allow overriding facility to in charge or head of the section to override the fund position while placing order keeping in view of the expected funds. This flexibility helps to process orders without interruption when the approvals/grants are delayed. This overriding facility can be used to override fund limits, price restrictions, expenditure limits, claim action date, cancellations date etc.

2.3.5. Search and display Function

The user should be able to search using keywords,

control numbers as well as search using phrases or words derived from retrieved records. Use of Boolean operators, alphabetical searching should be possible. Search system supporting the use of relational operators such as "< = > *(smaller than, equal to, greater than)*" in numerical chronological fields is desired.

Data should have minimum of coded data to make more user friendly and user prone.

A catalogue entry should have all related items together such as author, title, place of publication, publisher, and year of publication when the patron searches the catalogue for an item.

The search for a title should be able to show the status and sort the records alphabetically. If a search for a vendor is made it should retrieve all the titles of that vendor by keeping the vendor's name on the top with the order number and the code of the vendor while displaying.

2.3.6. Reports

The system should support report generation online or in batch mode. Some reports are generated by default while some are generated on demand. Acquisition default reports are recommendations, orders placed, items received, and invoices processed, claims and cancellations made, orders, invoice, fund records created and sorted by staff as per fund, vendor, subject or patron. Financial reports such as accounts payable, cash flow analysis, cost projections, fund status, fund transfer, invoices paid, foreign exchange reports, vendor performance, system performance, database use statistics are some of the reports can be created on demand. For this, we need to have flexible report generator, which will instruct the system in designing the report as required.

2.4. SIGNIFICANCE OF AUTOMATING ACQUISITIONS

In any acquisition system, there is need to maintain several paper files, e.g., on-order file, recommendations file, receipts file, file of orders placed, vendor correspondence, file of currency conversion rates, etc. Considerable effort is needed to maintain such files in manually maintained system and ensure that required action is done e.g. sending reminders for unsupplied items is taken promptly. In manual systems, the information required to be stored redundantly in different entries/ files. Searching for information in paper files can be time-consuming, error-prone and does not produce effective results. Automation can help reduce the drudgery and error-proneness of manual paper-based systems of maintaining files.

The acquisitions system of a library requires that the data created during the acquisition operations are shared with other subsystems, to improve the efficiency of the other subsystems, minimize data redundancy and in ensuring consistency. Automation could greatly help in this, e.g., cataloguing, circulation control, serials, etc

There is also need for overall efficiency in different processes involved in the acquisitions function, viz., request verification, ordering, receiving and verification of orders, follow-up, cancellation, etc. Automation can help improve the efficiency of these operations by ensuring that they are done as per schedule.

An important thing for automating the acquisitions function is the possibility for the preparation of useful management information reports, i.e., reports that would enable the senior and middle management of the library to take meaningful decisions in the interest of the library. Such reports can be processed and retrieved only if the data files used in acquisitions are up-to-date, which is better done in an automated system than in manual systems. There is a constant need to search for status of an item ordered, invoice received/forwarded for payment or any information concerning ordered material by library staff as well as users. In other words, library staff or users keep searching the files of the acquisitions system to retrieve information and if necessary take follow-up action. For instance, when a user asks information about the order status of the recommended item for the library, it is necessary to search on-order file. Searching a manual on-order file can be time-consuming and sometimes may not produce correct retrieval; because the searcher's request could not match the way the manual file is ordered.

Good management of acquisition of material requires that there is accuracy in all facets of the acquisitions processes, e.g., the accurate and timely financial data recording, accounting and reporting. Automated systems are obviously better equipped managing the operations to be more timely and accurate than the manual systems.

An important requirement in acquisitions management in automated environment is effective and be able to track orders, receipts, invoices and handle claims and also the cancellations of orders for the unsupplied items.

2.5. THE AUTOMATED ACQUISITION SYSTEM

The Automated Acquisition System relieves professionally qualified staff to concentrate more on the quality and content of acquisitions work rather than on the clerical work. An automated system, redundant operations are taken care by the computer and professional staff can learn more and try to work for the quality of acquisition operations. This does reduce the time available for them to concentrate on the qualitative aspects of acquisitions work. In manual systems of acquisition, the tasks are repetitive, time consuming, tedious for professional staff. Automation can improve the efficiency and reduce the redundancies of the information and work flows involved in acquisitions work

Infrastructure : By infrastructure it is meant that the pre-requisites and support structures required for an automated acquisitions system. These are as follows:

2.5.1. External Databases - Sources of Information

- On CD ROM's (Books In Print, publisher's catalogues, etc.)
- Through internet using online search systems.

- Online library catalogues and networks e.g., OCLC, Library of Congress
- Library networks, e.g. DELNET, INFLIBNET
- Publishers/Vendors/Intermediary Agencies
- Internal databases and files
- Central database

2.5.2. Retrieving Records from External Databases

The staff should be able to download the bibliographic data from external databases, such as - publisher web sites, online books in print or any other catalogues that support Z39.50 protocols for consistency and uniformity of records and to avoid redundancy in entering the data repeatedly. The data from other free online catalogues or union catalogues of OCLC by acquiring membership can be imported to enter bibliographic records for further processing of orders etc.

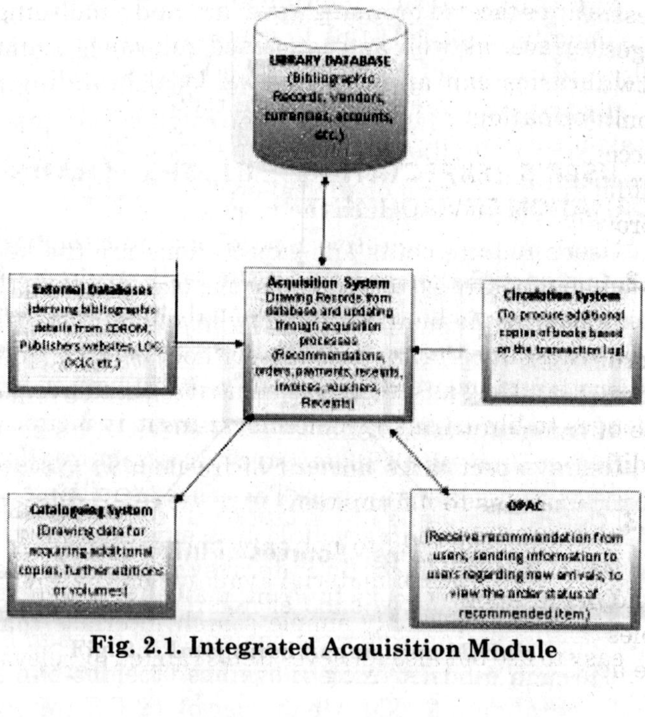

Fig. 2.1. Integrated Acquisition Module

2.5.3. Connecting to Internal databases

An acquisition system requires access to several local files and databases. The following internal files and databases are needed by an acquisitions system. The internal files are created and maintained by the library staff. Each record is assigned a unique identification number by the system, which identifies the record and links it with other records within and also other files in database. For example when the order number is typed it retrieves all the records linked to that order so that any item in that order can be received or given receipt status once the book is received.

2.6. ACQUISITION FILES AND RECORDS

2.6.1. User / Membership Files

These records are created as part of the circulation system. Access to these files is required in the acquisitions subsystem, to enable dissemination of information about new accessions to registered patrons or to process the lists of suggestions for approval to authorities. Usually the LIS software's provide permissions to users to send recommendations for books and other material; and the staff to access the circulation membership files (patron records of staff/faculty) to process the recommendations for placing for approvals and then orders.

2.6.2. Currency Exchange Rate Files

The data elements in this file will contain, currency record name, number, type, exchange rate, date, source of information (GOC), Staff member's (who has created) code, date of record created (system supplied), date of the record modified (system supplied), etc.

2.6.3. Online Catalogue of the Library

In the library, this file gives information on the bibliographic details of each specific item, the number of copies available for a specific item and its physical status. The acquisition, cataloguing and circulation modules of the automated library system share the central database. The data elements in the online catalogue shared by the acquisition module are: catalogue record identification number, author, corporate author, title, publisher, publication date, place of publication, edition, ISBN, no of volumes, number of pages, type of material, language of the item, edition number, broad subject area, keywords, classification number, accession number, parts number, copy number etc.

2.6.4. Authority Files

The files contain personal names, corporate names and addresses of corporate authors, publishers, vendors etc. This file validates the names and addresses during current acquisition processes to ensure accuracy and consistency. The authority files maintained are sharable across different modules. The data elements of these files are - authority record identification number, name, designation, corporate name, host organization name, address, street name, city, district, state, country, pin-code, telephone number, email address, website of parent organization, representation of the vendor for specific publishers, their subject specialization, policies of some international organizations to distribute some of their publications free of cost, policies of gifts exchange etc, operators name/ code, date record created, date record modified.

2.6.5. On Order/ In-Process File

This file contains all order records, records for materials received and records for materials still under processing. It contains working orders, items received, non-receipts, invoices received, claims made. The data elements of this file contain - order record number, catalogue record number containing author title publisher etc, order number, order date, status, requested number, source identification number (vendor/publisher record number), price, foreign currency, discount, funds affected, receipt date, item identification number invoice date, invoice control number, payment due date, claims date, notes, operators name, date record created, and last modified.

2.6.6. Order History File

All completed orders are transferred to the order history file which helps to know the performance of the vendor in supplying the books and it is removed from the on order/ in process file. The data elements are same as on order in process file.

2.6.7. Invoice Data File

The data elements of this file contain invoice record control number, invoice number, invoice date, date received, source (vendor), library order number, completeness code, item identification number, quantity of each item, unit price, discount, postage, foreign currency, item receipt date, total funds utilized, payment authorization, date of payment, cheque number, claims for outstanding items, invoiced but not received, notes, operators name/code, date record created, date record modified.

2.6.8. Financial Data File

This includes data elements of financial records such as- identification number, type of financial record, accounts payable, accounts receivable, status of fund whether available or completed, fund name, fund code, fund year, initial allocation, carry over allocation, source of carry over, expenditure limit, accounts receivable, accounts payable, allocation, status of accounting record, total amounts spent on shipping postage, etc, previous year accounting data, transfer of funds restriction on the use of any fund, notes, operators name, code, date record created, date record modified.

2.6.9. Vendor Data File

This file includes the names and addresses of the vendors approved for libraries for placing orders. Information about the publishers represented and the subjects that vendors may be specializing may also be included in the file and branches of the vendors will be included. This file may be part of the name and address authority file. The latest vendor records include mobile numbers of the contact persons, e-mail addresses, bank account details to transmit orders, claims, payments etc electronically, which would minimize the time in correspondence, amount transfers etc.

In an automated acquisitions system, the above-mentioned files (except the online catalogue, authority files and user/Membership files) are created and updated in the automated acquisitions module.

2.7. SUBSYSTEMS

The functions of acquisition division of the library can be analyzed different, but sequential operations, which are related to each other. Similarly, the automated acquisitions system could be broken down into several subsystems based on the discrete functions that are required to be performed. A typical automated acquisitions system will have the following functional subsystems:

- Processing Requests Received
- Duplicate checking
- Data entry for Ordering and updating
- Order production and transmission
- Received items processing
- Accessioning
- Invoice processing
- Reminders for unsupplied items or non-receipts
- Cancellation
- Physical preparation
- Financial records, budgeting and reporting
- Search and retrieval
- Management information reporting

2.8. WORK FLOW

It is important to reiterate that although we talk of subsystems, there is tight integration and data exchange that is constantly taking place between these subsystems in an integrated library automation system. For instance, when a new publication is added to the on order file, the financial records subsystem receives the data about the cost of the publication to be ordered and it then automatically updates the expenditure data as illustrated vide figure 2.2.

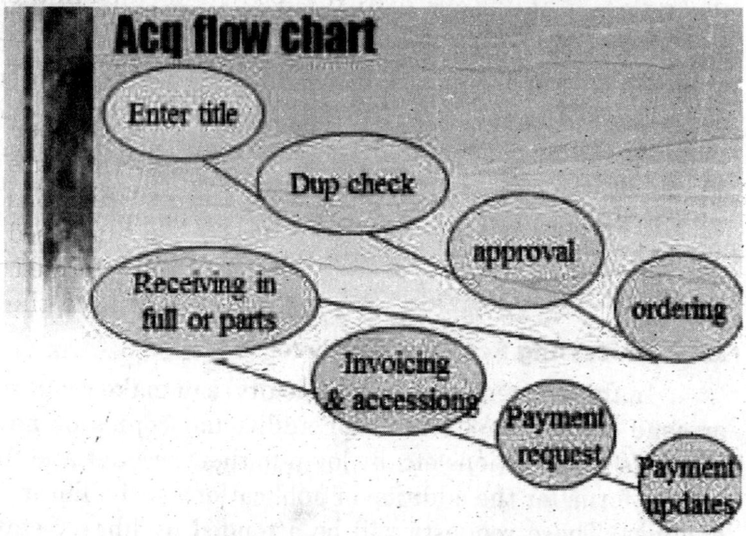

Fig. 2.2. Flow chart of Acquisitions Work

The typical features of each of these subsystems are described below.

2.8.1. Duplicate checking

Duplicate checking is done for knowing the availability of same item in the library and also to estimate the number of additional copies to be procured. Though it is very much essential, it is obviously time taking task, which needs additional effort. Certain libraries are making the task easier by executing additional programs. A recent incident of executing such an application is noted hereunder. Now a days to save the time in duplicate checking a script is prepared using PHP to detect procured titles from a list provided in Excel with n number of authors and titles together. It is tested with integrated library system KOHA database. Before executing the program an excel sheet is prepared containing two columns with author and title. It is saved as "booklist.xlsx" on desktop. While running the program using the address http:// localhost/duplicate/.the excel file is uploaded and by clicking on the check the duplicate link, the matching results will appear with link. For this installation of PHP Excel from website https:// phpexcel.codeplex.com/ is needed and it needs to be saved on desktop. Further, by right clicking the file it is to be decompressed in the same location and start copying the contents of the 'classes' folder to any required location in our application. Next a subfolder "duplicate 'can be created with write permissions. The excel file can be uploaded for duplicate checking. This saves the time for duplicate checking of titles in acquisitions.

2.8.2. Processing Requests Received

In this the registered user (faculty) can make requests or send suggestions online for additional copies or new products subscriptions etc. by login to their account and fill out the form, for the addition of publications to the library's holdings. These requests will be attended by library staff concerned and place order subject to the availability of funds and approvals. The requests are permitted through emails to the head of the acquisition department if available the librarian sends back the availability of the copy to the user through mail instantly. The budget account is also specified against which it should be booked.

The request processing subsystem supports the following functionalities:

- Permits instant messaging and/or email so that users are informed, for instance when a Publication suggested is already on order.
- Permit the searching of the on order file and library

catalogue to avoid duplication.

- Permit the online submission of lists for approval before purchase orders can be placed

2.8.3. Data entry for ordering and updating

When a library desires to acquire a publication, it is necessary that the data for the publication is entered (or imported) into its files. Further, the automated system should permit different library material and following types of acquisition. The system should support the gifts, and standing orders for annually published book series. For gifts the acknowledgement letter should also be generated simultaneously once gift books are entered. Further it should also allow pre-payments (advance payments) and post-orders (placing orders after receiving books and bills).

The order entry should be done by importing the data elements from online catalogues, books in print or from Library of congress easily.

There should be minimal key-in of data during data entry. This improves efficiency and minimizes errors.

The order data entry and updating module should also permit duplication checking when a new item is entered. This is checked against the on order file as well as the online catalogue to avoid unintended duplication, which is done automatically and the library staff will be alerted with the indication of duplication entry. The staff then has the option then to cancel the data entry of the item or override the alert and proceed entering the data for additional copies.

The data gets validated as and when it is entered by the authority files so created. The data entry can be modified if any mistakes take place by choosing the modify or edit option. This is only before the order is transmitted. Once the order is sent the system assumes that the order is sent to the vendor and does not allow for modifications.

2.8.4. Order Production and Transmission

Orders can be transmitted either online or through batch mode by producing orders and transmitting periodically. Orders can be sent through e mail of the vendor if the email is configured in the vendor directory created. It can sent through printed form.

This subsystem will also ensure that the on order files, financial records files are updated which are transparent to the user.

2.8.5. Received Item Processing

The received item processing subsystem ensures the efficient processing of received items. Through order number, it is possible to track the titles received by giving them the received status. This is usually done by searching the on order file by order number, usually a unique number assigned by the user or generated by the software at the time of order placement. However, if the order number is not available then it should be possible to retrieve by author or title of the item or by vendor. Once the appropriate record is retrieved, the receiving function allows the staff to enter details of the invoice, copies supplied, cost price of the item, currency in which the cost is invoiced, etc. Once this is done, the module registers the fact that the item was received on that date, updates the financial records, and creates a record in the order history file.

In a majority of the cases, the receiving function is straight forward, i.e., the item is received along with an invoice. But in some cases it should support if the item is received but not an invoice for it. An invoice is received but not the item. The order is partially supplied, e.g. out of 6 volumes only 3 are received. To handle damaged items to be returned to the vendor. The Receiving Item Processing subsystem should be capable of handling the above-mentioned exceptions.

Additionally, the subsystem should support the following:

Receive multiple volumes in a single transaction

- To enter receipt of damaged copies
- To return damaged copies to the vendor
- To accommodate receipt of gifts and exchanges
- To inform user who suggested the item/s for purchase
- To post discounts/to convert foreign currencies into payable currency
- To distribute postage over items
- To be able to handle advance payments (pre-payments)
- To make adjustments against advance payments.
- To handle post-orders (placing orders after receiving books and invoices)

2.8.6. Invoice processing

The user is allowed to enter the details of the invoice using the keyboard. This subsystem should allow the recording of single title, multiple title and partial shipment invoices. An important output of this subsystem is a printed or electronic authorization for the payment of the invoice.

2.8.7. Accessioning

After the item is received, accessioning is done by assigning a unique accession number in the order of sequence to the item received, while recording the other bibliographic details of the item, its source of supply, cost paid, budget debited, date of receipt, etc. most of the automated systems make provision to produce the accession number automatically or to be manually assigned by the library staff. If the accession number assigned or generated for each item is unique, the same can be used in circulation control to retrieve records for checkout, check-in operations.. Since the details of the item have already been captured in earlier functions, the process of accessioning in an automated system is simply to add a new record with the accession number to an accessions file. In some libraries, however, audit and statutory requirements force the library to maintain a separate accession register. Because of this an automated acquisition system should allow the printing of the accession register.

2.8.8. Reminders

This system should be able to schedule the lead time for supply or ordered items, at the vendor level, e.g. either 90 days or 60 days. It should be set in a way that after the specified period, the claims can be transmitted to the respective vendor/s or title wise. This subsystem can be configured to produce claims automatically, e.g., at the beginning of each week or on demand or at periodical intervals.

2.8.9. Cancellations

The order can be cancelled, reordered with another vendor. The subsystem should support the following functions:

- Cancellation of entire orders. The cancellation should be reflected in the fund account.
- Cancellation of part of orders.
- Re-issue of orders without re-entering order data.
- After cancellation of order, the system should automatically handle in a way presenting the receipt of cancelled items.
- Printing of cancellation notices.

2.8.10. Physical Preparation

Once the item is received and accessioned, the barcode labels are generated for accession numbers to physically paste on the item. Additionally, wherever necessary, the software should allow on demand the printing of assorted numbers on barcode labels for any given item in the library's collection.

2.8.11. Financial Records, Budgeting and Reporting

An important requirement in any acquisitions system

is the management of allocation of accounts, funds and the preparation of financial statements and reports. The allocation of funds to different budget heads is done at the beginning of each financial year but could be reallocated anytime.

It should also be possible to view the allocation of funds department wise, fund wise or year wise.

This subsystem must also provide the means to produce default reports, e.g., expenditure and balance statements, by budget head, funding source or publication type or vendor. So it should be possible to reallocate funds, creation of new funds, closing or deleting of funds, modifying or transferring amount from one fund to another.

2.8.12. Search and Retrieval

In this automated acquisition system the user should be able to track the order to know the status of the book recommended or ordered or received or in-process. So that a user will be able to send a reminder to library for executing the order. The items recommended can be searched in different files using title, order number, and to see when it was ordered and when it was received. If the vendor sends a letter stating that he is unable to supply the status can updated in the system and reordering can be thought of.

2.8.13. Performance Report to the Management

Automation should not only improve efficiency of operations, it should help in effective decision making process. Financial statements giving expenditures and balances available in different budget heads at any point of time.

- How a fund is used, spent and unspent amount.
- Amount spent by subject, department type of fund etc.
- Vendor performance reports. How many books he has supplied during a period of 3 months, Is he effective in supply or he is a poor supplier etc.

- The Report Writer in the software provides the interface and tools for library managers to define and create ad-hoc reports.

2.9. SHARING OF DATA WITH OTHER LIBRARY AUTOMATION SUBSYSTEMS

The acquisition system should be able draw the data for ordering from the online catalogue of the library.

- Acquire information from cataloguing system for additional copies to be ordered.
- Share the data with OPAC to show the status of the book.
- Must permit users to send requests by viewing acquisitions files via the OPAC
- Circulation system - circulation statistics will help to acquire additional copies of a book.
- Generating new books list monthly or weekly and providing a link in the web page that help the users to know the new arrivals.

Acquisition of information material is usually the beginning of library operations, which is followed by further processes of cataloguing, circulation etc. It is true with newly establishing libraries, but in an integrated automated environment, there will be a grave necessity of computerizing the existing collection, independent to acquisition operation.

While computerizing established libraries both the acquisition and retro-conversion /cataloguing operations need to be planned simultaneously. In the forthcoming chapters cataloguing and retro conversion are discussed.

3
Automation of Cataloguing Processes

3.1. INTRODUCTION

Automation of cataloguing module contributes the significant part in design and formation of the central data base. The central data base constitutes the principle component of the integrated library systems. MARC was tested by Library of Congress by mailing test tapes to 16 libraries in USA in 1966. The feedback from libraries helped them to deliver MARC II which was machine readable catalogue format for international exchange of catalogue as well as bibliographic data and modifications were made to standardize the format as per the machine requirements. MARC II began in 1968 and by 1973 records for serials maps and French books were added and by 1975 German, Spanish and Portuguese materials records were added. It was a subscription service by the Library of Congress. MARC format was developed in countries like Canada, Latin America, Spain, Denmark, Australia, Japan, France, Germany, Belgium and Switzerland. The multiplicity of these formats made it difficult to exchange machine readable data internationally. So the IFLA group on content designators formed in 1973 took steps to establish what is called UNIMARC which could facilitate translation of records and international exchange of data. This ISBD (International Standard Bibliographic Description) standard formed the basis of UNIMARC with full content designation for all data elements.

Online catalogues could provide machine readable files in MARC for transferring from the magnetic tape to the magnetic disc or drum where random access was possible. Visual display units were used for input output operations and these terminals were connected to the printer for hardcopy output. Library of Congress defined online catalogues as "an access tool and resource guide to the collections of the library or libraries which contains interrelated sets of bibliographic data in machine readable form and which can be searched interactively on a terminal by users."

3.2. NEED FOR AUTOMATION OF CATALOGUING

The need for computerization of library operations has been felt due to the ever-increasing workload in libraries in all spheres. A computerized cataloguing system can facilitate the following:

- To increase the efficiency
- To achieve speed in cataloguing
- Economy of staff and services
- Improved updating of the catalogue
- Variety of outputs
- Possible to input more bibliographical details
- To be able to handle depth subject cataloguing
- There is a scope for multiple access to files through online
- Improved information accessibility through increased access points
- Speed in locating and retrieving information

- Search of items by combination of index terms

3.3. THE ROLE OF CATALOGUING:

Cataloguing is the most important function of the library. The catalogue may be called as central database as it shares the records across all the modules in the library automation system. To share the bibliographic record and avoid duplication of records consistency and standardization is important. To exchange bibliographic records there should be a common format such as MARC 21. Now a day's most of the software vendors follow MARC 21 standards. The data structures should represent the catalogue data in automated cataloguing systems. The retrospective conversion issues in converting manual catalogue records to machine-readable form need to be addressed and the methods followed in such conversion are discussed in this chapter.

The catalogue is undoubtedly library's most valuable resource. It is the result of careful and painstaking descriptive and analytical work. Importantly, cataloguers need to apply exacting standards and use standard tools in their descriptive and analytical work. A good catalogue should maintain accuracy, completeness and consistency with which a library's holdings are described, classified and indexed. The primary purpose of the catalogue is to provide easy and effective access to the library's collection for the effective retrieval of information, to meet needs of the library users.

The catalogue is the interface to the database and it is a collection of many related and interacting files. The catalogue in an automated library is also the central database because all other subsystems of the library draw their information from the catalogue. Much of the functionality of different subsystems of a library depends on the availability of the catalogue as a searchable database.

The cataloguing and classification operations involve considerable intellectual effort of highly trained professionals. However, automation can and does relieve professionals of routine and redundant tasks (e.g., sorting and filing of cards, keyboarding of data), and in helping to achieve standardization and uniformity. By automation a library's collection is more widely and easily accessible to its patrons.

3.4. SIGNIFICANCE OF AUTOMATING THE CATALOGUING OPERATIONS

Cataloguing, classification and subject indexing are among the costliest processes in a library since these operations require highly trained personnel. Cataloguing costs are much higher than any other costs in the library, since most of the libraries in developing countries do original cataloguing. An important justification for automating the cataloguing function in a library is to see how it could help in reducing costs of cataloguing books. This is possible primarily through the sharing of catalogue records over networks and by using machine-readable cataloguing data from Library of Congress or Library networks of OCLC. Only when a library has an automated catalogue can get the benefit of catalogue records that are available on library networks and the Internet.

If a library depended entirely on original cataloguing, It is estimated that, a cataloguer can catalogue a maximum of 10 to 12 books in a day, depending on the level of description given in cataloguing and in standards that are followed by the library. In a large library, total dependence on original cataloguing for new books acquired by the library could take one month before they become available to users. The time lost by potential users is loss of opportunity and delay in getting the information. Hence, it is very much necessary to reduce the time it takes to make new books available to users.

The most compelling reason for automating the cataloguing function of a library (and access to its catalogue) is to make available the catalogue to users over the local area network (LAN) of the organization and to remote users via the Internet. Now more and more organizations are getting into networks and the users are accustomed in searching information through their computer devices and expect information delivery to their desktops or any other devices. This is imperative for libraries to automate their catalogues.

Another important reason for automation of cataloguing books, journals etc is to avoid the unnecessary duplication in intellectual cataloguing effort that takes place when the same title is catalogued repeatedly. If these efforts are shared it will bring a cost reduction plus making the reading material available to the user more quickly. Moreover, the cataloguing function is the possibility, for obtaining greater accuracy, completeness and consistency in a library's catalogue, which requires utmost care in manual cataloguing. If a library decides to use the cataloguing data from an authoritative source, e.g., the national library of the country or an international source such as the Library of Congress or an international cooperative network such as OCLC, standardization and uniformity can be achieved. Using their cataloguing data would add value and quality to a local library catalogue. Automation of the cataloguing function allows a library to contribute their records to a national, regional or international cooperative networks. It is only through such cooperative efforts that the intellectual output of institutions will be known all over the world and accessible globally.

More and more digital resources, including full text and multimedia are becoming available on organizational networks and on the Internet. Library catalogues are expected to provide access, not only to conventional resources but also to a host of web-based ones that are useful to a library's clients.

Automating the cataloguing function enables the metadata that a catalogue provides to link with the respective other resources within the library and beyond, particularly on the Internet. For instance, a catalogue record of a book could have a URL (Universal Resource Locator) of a web site that provides abstracts of papers in the publication (e.g., conference proceedings). Similarly, it is possible to add value to an automated catalogue record by attaching an image of the cover page, contents page of the publication in question. It is also possible to link the record to a digitized full-text version of the publication through metadata, the digitized version resides on the organization's network or in external web site.

Automation in cataloguing can bring the best benefits to staff and users only when the library follows international standards. Newer standards such as (e.g., the Z39.50 and the ISO-ILL Protocols) allows even greater inter-communication and interoperability via the Internet and the web. One of the major advantage of using Z39.50 is that it enables uniform access to a large number of diverse and heterogeneous information sources.

The automated catalogue functions relieve staff from dependence on physical files, especially the card catalogue. As a result the staff will be able to use the subject knowledge more effectively, regardless of their physical location. Language and subject expertise of the staff can be used for specialized works as the respective staff members will be possessing knowledge in their area. For instance, music recordings can be ordered, received and catalogued in a music library, if the staff are possessing skills. Some staff members may have several types of responsibilities and are experts in executing different tasks. By taking their expertise, the library can conduct training programs in specific procedures and records, instead of sending juniors out for even small issues. By coordination this can be achieved at best (Schwartz, 1998)

Automation has made libraries to reconsider the technical workflow of technical operations and possible to trace, what was done modify, when it was done, who did it, and whether it was done piece by piece or in batch. Staff responsibilities have changed so that professionals spend more time on management, while all levels of staff have acquired more skills, often being cross-trained for a variety of jobs that require a similar knowledge base (Buttlar and Garcha, 1998). Hence the staff can be used for multiple functions without appointing additional staff members.

Vendors now have come up with shelf ready material (resources) with catalogue-ready records for libraries who make a commitment to purchase in advance. The availability of records gives an opportunity for libraries to use the services provided by ILS vendors through software package.

3.5. COMPUTERIZED CATALOGUING STANDARDS & FORMATS

So it is important for libraries to develop catalogue in machine readable form in the frame work of international data exchangeable formats and standards. So that the bibliographic data can be shared worldwide for the use of scholars, researchers or even a layman over coming all the barriers such as incompatible formats. These formats are standardized by the international organizations viz. International Standard Organization (ISO), National Information Standard Organization (NISO), and National level organizations, etc

ISO/IEC guide 2:1996 defines a standard as a document established by consensus and approved by a recognized body that provides for common and repeated use, rules and guidelines or characteristics for activities or their results aimed at the the achievement of the optimum degree of order in a given context. Library standards are documented agreements containing technical specifications or other precise criteria to be used consistently as rules guidelines or definitions of characteristics to ensure those materials products, processes and services are fit for their processes. Gautham and Singh (2003) categorized bibliographic formats as two kinds -

1. Working formats : the bibliographic formats that satisfy the specific requirements of the national bibliographies and other national demands. E.g. UKMARC, USMARC, AUSMARC, INTERMARC, CANMARC, USMARC

2. Communication format : to be used for the exchange of bibliographic information from one national bibliography to another e.g. UNIMARC

3.5.1. Computer output microfilm (COM)

COM catalogue was developed as the outgrowth of book catalogue. The process begins by first converting the catalogue into machine readable form and it is stored in magnetic tape or disc or any other storage medium without creating a paper copy.

3.5.2. CD-ROM Catalogue

It is a catalogue contains a MARC based compilation of bibliographic records and distributed on CD ROM with accompanying software which helps to perform the following functions. Catalogues distributed in this format i.e. local public access catalogue, union catalogue support interlibrary loan, reference and also function as a database of bibliographic information or resource data file for extraction of records to use in retrospective conversion, card production and ongoing additions to a local online database .

3.5.3. Online Public Access Catalogue

Computerized cataloguing enabled online public access catalogue but not all online catalogues are public catalogues for eg it can be online facility for library staff and an offline microfiche catalogue for the user.

3.5.4. Common Communication Format (CCF)

CCF was developed by UNESCO within the framework of general information program. This could provide a standard and common method for structuring bibliographic records so that these records could be freely exchanged among different information systems.

3.5.5. Anglo American Cataloguing Rules (AACR)

AACR was popularly accepted and widely known in developing countries. They serve as the basis for the form and content of data entered in each field. Many of the standard bibliographic formats have used AACR rules for describing the bibliographic contents and form of the fields and this is used by many integrated library system vendors for structuring the bibliographic database. The evolution of MARC 21 format by library of congress is also based on AACR rules.

3.5.6. International Standard Bibliographic Description (ISBD)

The important aim of the ISBD was to provide a standard form of bibliographic description for exchanging records internationally. This would support IFLA's program of universal *bibliographic control*. This contains rules for providing bibliographic description of books and other materials to bring standardization by IFLA (*International Federation of Library Associations and Institutions*). In 2011 modifications were brought including *monographs*, older monographic publications, cartographic materials, serials and other continuing resources, electronic resources, non-book materials, and printed music.

https://en.wikipedia.org/wiki/International_Standard_Bibliographic_Description

3.5.7. Machine Readable Catalogue (MARC)

It is bibliographic records that are available in machine readable form. The structure of MARC records is an implementation of national and international standards, e.g., *Information Interchange Format* (ANSI Z39.2) and *Format for Information Exchange* (ISO 2709).MARC 21is a standard for representing and communication of bibliographic and its related information in machine readable form. Developed by LOC (Library of Congress) they are specifications of communication formats and used in exchange of bibliographic information and processing. A MARC 21 format is a set of codes and content designators defined for encoding machine-readable records. Formats are defined for five types of data: bibliographic, holdings, authority, classification, and community information. It is done in consultation with user communities.

3.5.8. UNIMARC

The UNIMARC Bibliographic format was first created and proposed by IFLA in 1977, with the title *UNIMARC: Universal MARC format*. This was to bring about international exchange of bibliographic database. It has a set of four formats such as Bibliographic, Authorities, Classification and Holdings - and related documentation.

3.5.9. UNICODE

Whatever be the program, platform or language Unicode provides a unique number for every character the standards of which has been adopted by big industries like Apple, HP, IBM, Just Systems, Microsoft, Oracle, SAP, Sun, Sybase, Unisys and *many others*. It is encoded in XML, JAVA, ECMAScript (Javascript), LDAP, COBRA 3.0, WML, etc thus implementing ISO/IEC 10646. This is supported by many operating systems and latest browsers and other modern products. The Unicode standards and its supporting tools are one of the most technology developments and every language can be entered in its original language and retrieval of bibliographic records is possible in the original language. Unicode facilitates single software across multiple platforms, languages and countries and enables data transfer through many systems without corrupting the data. When Unicode is incorporated into client –server or multi-tiered applications and websites, helps to achieve cost savings.

3.5.10. Dublin Core

Meta data means data about data. According to Wikipedia "the Dublin Core Schema is a small set of vocabulary terms that can be used to describe web resources (video, images, web pages, etc.), as well as physical resources such as books or CDs, and objects like artworks. The full set of Dublin Core metadata terms can be found on the Dublin Core Metadata Initiative (DCMI) website". Dublin Core Metadata may be used for multiple purposes, from simple resource description, to combining metadata vocabularies of different metadata standards, to provide interoperability for metadata vocabularies in the Linked Data cloud and Semantic Web implementations.

The Dublin Core Metadata Initiative, or "DCMI", is an open organization supporting innovation in metadata design. DCMI maintains a number of formal and informal liaisons and relationships with standards bodies and other metadata organizations for the development of interoperable online metadata standards for a broad range of purposes. The Dublin Core Schema is a small set of vocabulary terms that can be used to describe web resources (video, images, web pages, etc.), as well as physical resources such as books or CDs, and objects like artworks. The NISO Z39.85-2001 standard addresses the Dublin Core Element Set and defines 15 metadata elements for resource discovery.

These fifteen fields of the record according to Dublin Core are –

1. Title
2. Author or creator
3. Subject and key words
4. Description
5. Publisher
6. Other contributor
7. Date
8. Resource type
9. Format
10. Resource identifier
11. Source

12. Language
13. Relation
14. Coverage
15. Rights management

The Dublin Core standard originally includes two levels: Simple and Qualified. Simple Dublin Core comprised 15 elements; Qualified Dublin Core included 3 additional elements (Audience, Provenance and Rights Holder), as well as a group of element refinements (also called qualifiers) that could refine the semantics of the elements in ways that may be useful in resource discovery. Since 2012 the two have been incorporated into the DCMI Metadata Terms as a single set using the Resource Description Framework (RDF).

3.5.11. Z39.50 Standard

Z39.50 is an international standard protocol for searching and retrieving information from a database in a TCP/IP Computer network. It is maintained by Library of Congress. It is a protocol for client-Server, application layer and communication. It is based on ANSI/NISO standard Z39.50, and ISO standard 23950. It is highly used in libraries and embedded into integrated library systems and personal bibliographic reference software. Z39.50 is implemented for searching catalogues for inter library loan purposes. It started in 1970 and has updated versions in 1992.95.98 and 2003. It was earlier called as Common Query Language.

It has two way communications and it works in the following way.

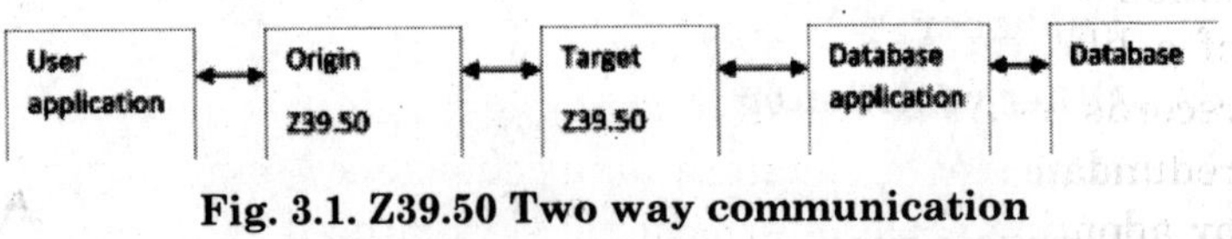

Fig. 3.1. Z39.50 Two way communication

3.5.12. International Development Information Network (IDIN)

They developed manual for use by small documentation centres using CDS/ISIS to create a bibliographic database and to provide services such as online search accession list, CAS bulletins, catalogues and indexes.

3.6. AUTOMATED CATALOGUING PROCESSES

Infrastructure means the pre-requisites and support structures for an automated cataloguing system. These are as follows:

- External databases - sources of bibliographic information
  - * Through Cataloguing resources on CD ROM's
  - * Through a Internet, e.g., to web sites of a national library
  - * Through online library catalogues
  - * Through library networks, service providers, e.g., OCLC
- Internal databases and files

3.6.1. Retrieving information from External Databases

The external databases can be used for automating the cataloguing function as a source of cataloguing and authoritative data. Such databases were available on a CD-ROM, and nowadays on the Internet, on a library utility such as OCLC. OCLC and commercial sites would obviously be available only to members or subscribers of their services. However, there are a number of library sites like Library of Congress that provide free access to their catalogue records and allow them to be downloaded. Similarly, access to the union catalogue of a library network or the online catalogue of a library that allows the downloading of cataloguing records would be useful in avoiding duplication of work and redundancy, while maintaining consistency and uniformity by adopting same international standards.

Works attended in cataloguing section are -

- Preparing catalogue cards for main entry, added entries, cross-reference entries, Preparing and maintaining authority files.

- Assigning subject headings using Sears's list of subject headings or Library of Congress Subject Headings.
- Assigning classification numbers (DDC, CCC, UDC etc.)
- Data entry through computer
- Retrospective conversion
- To update Online Public Access Catalogue
- A list of recent additions to display or distribute over LAN or internet or through group mail or link to library portal
- Preparing bar-coded labels.

The number of directory entries in the record is the same as the number of variable fields being described in the record. As a result the number of directory entries varies from one record to another. Therefore there is always a need to have the field called "Base address of data" in the Leader section of the MARC. The directory entries help the computer program to locate the required data in the catalogue data entry template of the software in use. The software that is used by the cataloguer to import one or more MARC records from an external source in the exchange format need to be placed for editing and adding local fields if required and saves it to the database The directory entries of the imported records are the ones permitting the software to locate and display the data imported into the software's data entry templates.

3.6.2. Control fields

The actual bibliographic data will be found in the control field and variable field sections of the record. Control fields are fixed fields and numbered from 001-008. Each one is terminated by a field terminator (FT). The details of the control field is given below.

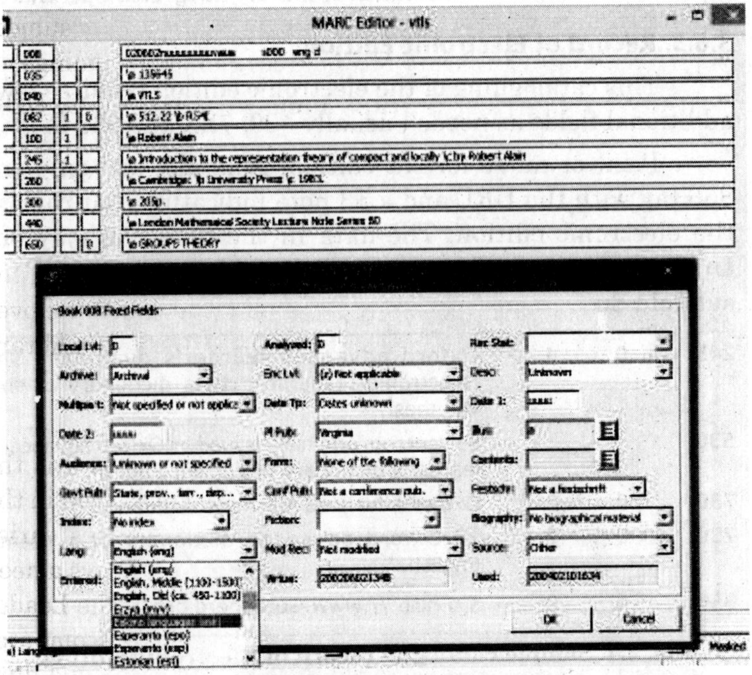

Fig. 3.2. Control Field

LDR			*Sample MARC record*
006			Fixed field
008			(Fixed field) 050227 000 0 eng d
082			$a 900 $b S45h
100	1		$a Robert, John, $d 1950.
245	1	0	$a E-Journals : $b a how to do manual/ $c By John Robert and Kim Kimberly
250	#	#	$a 2nd ed.
260	#	#	$a New York : $b Robert & Kimberly $c 1999
300	#	#	$ X, 100p. : $b ill; $c24 cm.
440	#	#	$a Manual text; $v no. 6
504	#	#	$a Includes bibliographical references.
600	1		$a Kimberly, Kim.
650	#	0	$a E-Journals.
856			/u: electronic location of a book
900			$a 1222

Fig. 3.3. Sample MARC Record

3.6.3. Record of Electronic Edition

This cataloguing of the electronic edition requires few additional fields as needed usually 530, 7XX and 856 fields.

Print or micro format edition: generally add only an 856 tag with the URL and a $3 note indicating that this is the electronic edition. The data in the field 856 may be Uniform Resource Identifier (URI), which is recorded in subfield $u

245	0	4	Oxford advanced learner's dictionary $h [electronic resource]: $b a dictionary of six volumes.
530			$a contents originally issued as Oxford advanced learner's dictionary of current English
730	0	2	Oxford advanced learner's dictionary.
730	0	2	$a Oxford advanced dictionary of current English.
856	4	0	$ u http:// www.Gutenberg.org

Fig. 3.4. Sample catalogue record of Electronic edition

Typical automated cataloguing system will have the following functional subsystems:

- Searching, retrieving and display of the record
- Data Entry
- Verification and validation of records
- Authority control
- Printing

It is important to reiterate that although we talk of subsystems, these are tightly integrated so that data exchange can take place between different subsystems in integrated library automation software. Data exchange takes place in a seamless or transparent manner for instance between the cataloguing data entry and authority control subsystems. The typical features of each of these subsystems are described as under :

3.6.4. Searching, Retrieving and Display of the Record

The records should be searched using multiple options such as author, title series, advanced search with keywords and using "And' or Not "Boolean operators. The searches made should be saved so that same terms can be resubmitted for further search. Alphabetical, numerical and publication date search should be allowed. Searches made should be narrowed with location, type of publication (book, serial, map, music score, computer files etc), physical format (print, disk, online) of the material, dates or languages etc.

Search facility should be possible across all the modules. The items displayed should have limited coded value. The author followed by title publisher, place of publication and year of publication should be together so that the user or the staff understands and easy to read it.

3.6.5. Data entry

In addition to the direct entry of bibliographic details in English language, the ILS should permit entering data in the other scripts (original) language by invoking a key which will enable to open virtual keyword in the respective language. The staff knowing the language script as well as keying-in computer on the language enabling virtual keyboard to enter the bibliographic data in the particular language. While following MARC 21 in cataloguing the original language script can be displayed with a connecting tag 880 for any field author, title or subject headings which can be retrievable. These other language entries can be made in addition to English for author/s' title, notes, and subject headings. The catalogue entry should also contain a URL which will enable them to connect to the full text document, abstract, table of contents etc. of a conference, any digital images link or contents page of a book.

3.6.6. Verification and Validation of records

The junior staff should first write the cataloguing data on worksheets which will be verified by the senior staff after which the data entry in the computer should be done. Validation takes place with the authority that gets built in when the name is rendered for the first time. It can also be checked with online authority files (LOC) after which it gets validated. When the ISBN is entered for the first time it gets validated.

3.6.7. Authority Control

Database in a machine readable form is an efficient, effective and economical way of maintaining authority file. MARC-21 format for Authority Data [http://www.loc.gov/MARC/authority/ecadhome.html]. LOC defines the authority record as: "a carrier for information concerning the authorized forms of names and subjects to be used as access points in MARC records, the forms of these names, subjects and subdivision to be used as references to the authorized forms and the interrelationships among these forms". A name may be used as he main, added, subject-added or series – added access entry. The term 'name 'refers to Personal names, corporate names, Meeting names, Names of jurisdictions, Uniform titles, Name/title combinations. A subject may be used only as a subject access entry. The term "subject' refers to Topical terms, Geographical, Names with subject subdivisions and Terms and names used as subject subdivisions.

Authority file is not necessary for small library whereas it is important for large libraries. It is better to have one's own authority file. Three types of authority files are commonly used are:

- **Name Authority file :** The Library of Congress Name Authority File (NAF) provides authoritative data for names of persons, organizations, events, places, and titles. Its purpose, is to provide uniform access to bibliographic resources through controlled vocabulary. This file is available in machine-readable format from the Cataloguing Distribution Service (CDS). Personal Name, Corporate Name, Conference or Meeting, Series title, Uniform title can be checked against this. When an author's name has to be rendered for the first time, the cataloguer has to decide the rendering and recording of the name. Such a rendering has to be recorded in an authority file for successive use.

- **Subject Authority File :** Library of Congress Subject Headings or the Sears list of subject headings. Sears's list of Subject Headings or LC subject headings can serve as authority file for subject headings. Looking into the subject and its nature, references have to be provided from broad to a narrow subject; from a subject to its division; from subject to its related subject. Such record has also to be maintained. A thesaurus or standard list of subjects, its sub divisions, and related ones can be maintained. Now a days such files are available online from the websites of Library of Congress for cross checking and rendering the correct one.
- **Series Authority (added entries) :** Authority records for series headings are created to ensure consistency in the use of these headings, as well as to provide increased access to library users through appropriate references in the catalogue, and to document the library's treatment practice for each series heading. Cataloguers should use care and judgment in deciding whether additional sources need to be checked before a heading can be established.

3.6.8. Printing

Printing catalogue cards or for printing accession register if it is necessary. Barcode labels can be generated. Spine labels can be printed. Some libraries print 5x3 catalogue cards according AACR2 and use it as shelf list cards. Call number wise printing can be done for conducing stock verification.

3.7. RETROSPECTIVE CONVERSION

In 1960 Library of Congress launched a pilot project on retrospective conversion. In this a record containing information about documents is referred as machine readable catalogues (MARC). This bibliographic information is prepared using a standard code such as AACR or LC.

Thus the process of converting the manual catalogue into machine readable form is known as Retrospective Conversion. One of the prerequisite in library automation is to create a database of in-house collection. Data entry is not a serious problem for small or new libraries as everything starts afresh but the bigger libraries will have a serious problem as the existing collection of different types of documents go beyond thousands and lakhs in number.

3.7.1. Types of Retrospective conversion

1. Full conversion: Retrospective conversion of the entire collection of the library.
2. Partial conversion:
   a. Documents that are in use
   b. Documents that are in circulation
   c. Documents of a particular subject
   d. Documents of a particular language
   e. Documents of a particular type like serials, textbooks etc.
   f. Documents of a particular media like microfilms, microforms etc.

3.7.2. Strategies for Retrospective Conversion

- Planning as in-house activity
- Taking it up as a project
- Outside agency contract
- Engaging additional manpower
- Conversion from CD-ROM databases by downloading the data..

- Conversion by using OCR (Optical Character Recognition).

3.7.3. Issues involved in Retro conversion

- Workflow designing
- Ensuring data input
- Data checking/verification
- Standardization – MARC, CCF, ISO Format
- Various methods have to be tried depending upon the size and infrastructure of the library.
- None of the methods are completely satisfactory.

So it is better to prepare work sheets and get it verified by professional staff and feed the data into the computer and errors should be rectified at the entry point.

Some libraries will be following UNESCO's CDS/ISIS (Computerized Documentation System - Integrated Set for Information Systems) to record bibliographic data and some others may have followed CCF (Common Communication Format) for recording bibliographic data. During automation the vendor's software will import these data from the import function which is leading to some inconsistencies. So it is always better to import into a common format ISO-2709 which supports MARC 21 and AACR2 and then import it into the vendor's integrated Library application software. While going in for Retro conversion it is necessary to begin with decisions

- Standards i-e follow AACR2 & MARC21
- Cut- off date the automation for starting, i.e. the year of publication of books or accession number or call number. This can be known through circulation statistics.

Secondly to decide whether we want to bring standardization and uniformity for which the library is moving to a different software for automation process.

From which section the automation process should start either from cataloguing or circulation or both at a time. The library should ensure that minimum storage space for the system, e.g. 2500 characters space for each title. In addition storage space for patron records, vendor directory, budget accounts, currency rates etc.

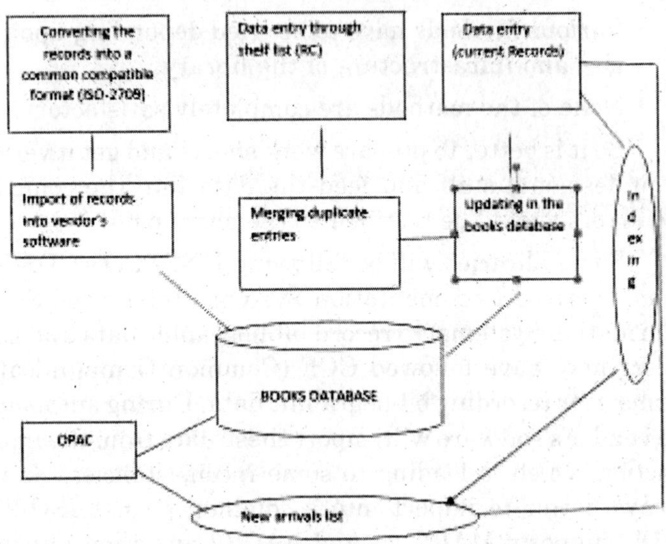

Fig. 3.5. Data Conversion from Manual to Automation

It is always better to go in for in-house operation by preparing work sheets which is verified by the senior and then data entry is done.

3.8. PROBLEMS ENCOUNTERED DURING AUTOMATION

- Usually bibliographic records entered during acquisition process are to be retrieved for cataloguing purpose by means of barcode numbers or title or author etc. Often double entries of same item occur when fresh entries are made through cataloguing module disregarding the acquisition records.

- The same accession number or barcode number may repeat for different title when manually assigning them to items. This can be rectified manually checking with the Accession register. This usually happens after the retro-conversion process. So it is always suggested to select serially assigned accession numbers for procured items in libraries.
- Sometimes data entry is done using articles as it is mentioned in title of the book or any other material, whereas articles are omitted. The situation leads to improper filing, indexing ultimately effects the retrieval. The condition which occurs in manual process can be refined during automation by selecting an option to "skip initial articles in indexing the entries"
- Hardware or power cut problems may cause loss of the data when it is not saved.
- Spelling, transliteration variations while entering data may lead to similar kind of problems in indexing which will be effecting retrieval, e.g.' Encyclopedia of library science' or' Encyclopaedia of library science' or missing a word etc. When software does not spell check or link these variations, cataloguer or data entry personnel may need to take care in linking these variations lest leading to duplication in procurement or missing the information during retrieval.
- Assigning different class number to same book copy/ different volume or edition received at later date in library may dislocate each specific item physically from the sequence.

The above cited issues in data entry are only few. Such wrong rendering of data would undoubtedly infect the database and effect the retrieval as illustrated in the following figure.

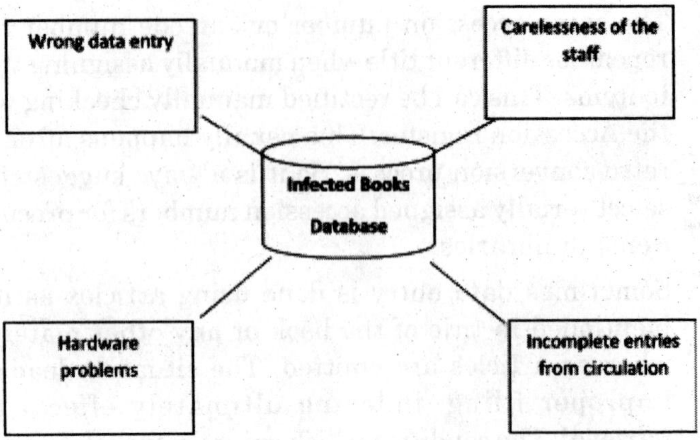

Fig. 3.6. Infected database

- Correction can be done by verifying with the accession register, with shelf list.
- By attending to user's complaint by correcting the necessary entries. Sometimes due to urgency in the process of automation books will be issued at the circulation with minimum details such as author and title. Such books when returned can be rectified by seeing the book.
- Improper entries such as wrong spelling or articles can be rectified by removing them. The same will be shown in the online public access catalogue.
- Class numbers for particular subjects and subdivisions need to be decided for standardization and uniformity.
- A manual containing all the specifications with regard to classification and cataloguing need to be prepared and the same has to be followed by all the staff working in the library. The manual will be a guiding source for future staff. It can also serve as an authority file.

The figure explains the same.

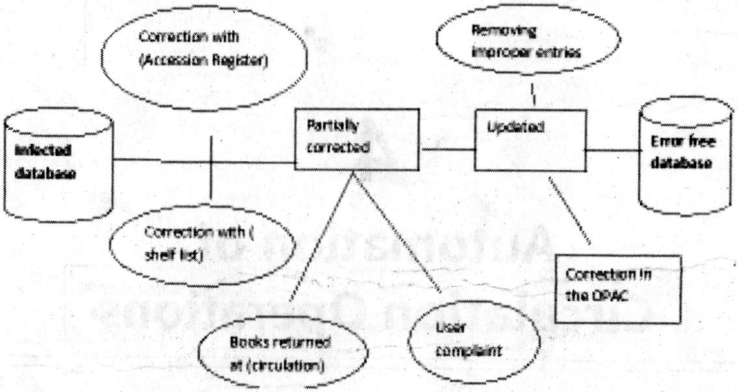

Fig. 3.7. Stages of correction

3.9. SHARING DATA WITH OTHER MODULES

Cataloguing is the central database. It captures minimum data from the acquisitions for creating full bibliographic record. It sends almost complete data to circulation for issue and return of books. It receives book requests from OPAC for ordering additional copies. It receives incomplete data either from circulation or when user returns the book to rectify the mistakes. Thus cataloguing module shares data with acquisition, circulation and OPAC.

Every software vendor designs their software based on bibliographic description and hence most of the LIS software's satisfy all the requirements of cataloguing module. Most of the software vendors follow MARC21 format for structuring their database allowing compatibility and thus facilitate exchange of bibliographic data across the modules within the system and across systems.

4

Automation of Circulation Operations

4.1. INTRODUCTION

The circulation operation was one of the initial attempts of library automation. The automation of circulation began in 1960's in western countries, using large computers aiming to meet the requirements of the users with regard to borrowed information of reading materials. The effort was proved very expensive, though this system was made user centred. Automation is considered as the most important as users directly interact with library for books and other materials.

Circulation systems in the earlier times were batch processed systems. The minicomputers and visual display terminals made easy the storage of circulation transactions easier on disk drives. Moreover, the impact of automation is more visible in circulation and online catalogue.

4.2. NEED FOR AUTOMATED CIRCULATION SYSTEM

The foremost important aspect of automation of circulation system is its efficiency to provide transactions as well as defaulters data to management and circulation status of the books to users. The manual system of circulating books, i.e. issues, renewals and return of books, filing of book cards after issues and removal of right cards at the time of returning to library is a lengthy and time-consuming process in large libraries. In addition, these process prone to errors in the circulation transactions, e.g. retrieval of wrong cards and inserting the same into the book which is different. While the same book is issued to a borrower, it creates havoc at the time of return because of the wrong card. In such situations, a computerized circulation system maintains all the user transactions and book transactions systematically and accurately. Sending reminders for overdue books manually is a very tedious task as number of registers, cards should be handled for sending reminders and for their rearrangement. In a computerized system this job is done easily without much effort as the machine maintains all the data which can searched by using different options such as due date and patron records for sending overdue notices.

Circulation also provides transactions data by which library can assess the demand for books, e.g. those are highly used or reserved. The library can also know the less used books and such books if not used for longer period may be decided for weeding out or moving them to passive collection. The circulation transaction data help to present such facts to the library committee for taking appropriate decision regarding unused books or other material.

4.3. BASIC FUNCTIONS OF AN AUTOMATED CIRCULATION SYSTEM

The automated circulation system should be able to perform the following functions for the easy process.

- To be able to retrieve membership records from library database.
- Be able to access online catalogue of the library while charging and discharging circulation functions.

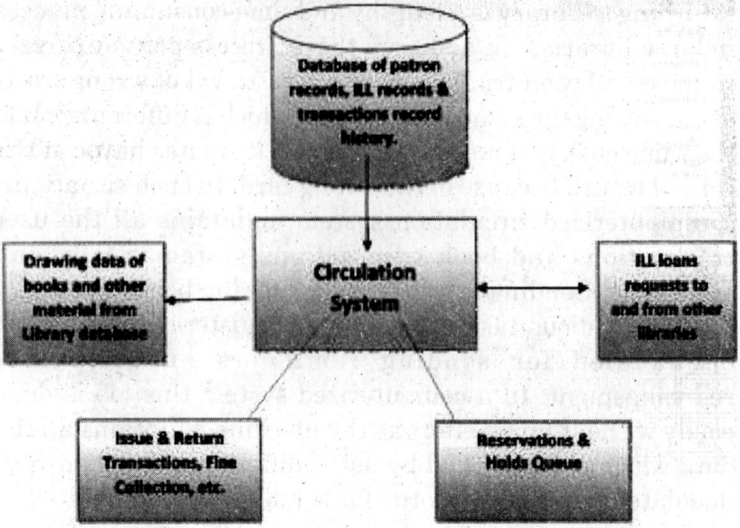

Fig. 4.1. Integrated Circulation System

- Be able to provide information regarding the privileges in connection to different types of circulated material to the categories of members such as students, faculty, guest faculty, research scholar & other students.
- The system should be able to get information regarding fines to be charged based on the category of patrons and the fine amount that should be charged.
- Circulation system should be compatible to the barcode equipment for printing the receipts of over dues collections and for scanning a barcode of patron ID or book Item barcode (accession number).

4.3.1. Data Structure of Patron Record

Patron record is the basic component in circulation system. The figure 4.2 illustrates the various fields (tags) and subfields in MARC format.

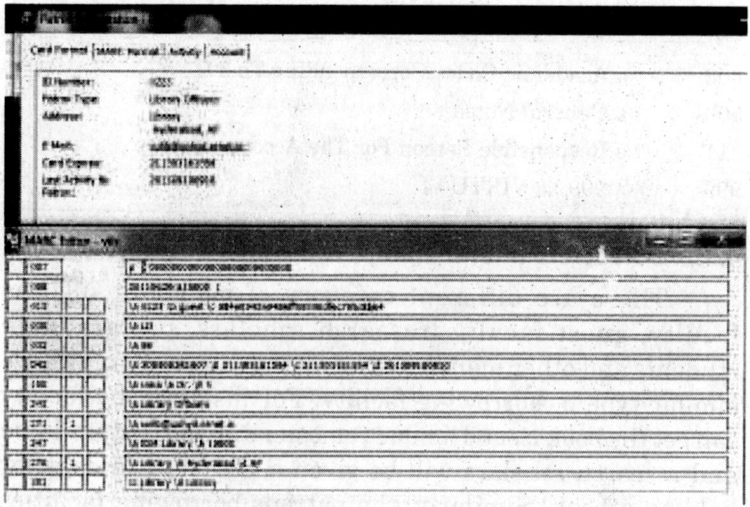

Fig. 4.2. Screenshot of Patron Record

The details of fields and subfields are described vide the following table.

Table 4.1. Patron Record – Important fields and subfields

Tag No	*Description*
015	\a Patron ID \b Password
030	\a Patron Type Code
032	\a Circulation Count
042	\a Registration Information Start Date \b Expiration Date and Time \c Automatic Deletion Date and Time \d Last Activity Date and Time
100	\a Patron Name \d Date of Birth \e Prefix \s Gender
245	\a Patron Type Description For 030
247	\a IGM Library \b Code if any
270	\a Address in 5 Lines \b City \d State \e PIN Code \f India \j Specialized telephone \k Telephone
271	\a Email
301	\a University of Hyderabad \c School \d Department \e Class

302	\a Academic Codes Corresponding To 301
500	\a General Notes
711	\a Responsible Person For The Account Holder
999	\a 999 \a VIRTUA4

4.3.2. Borrowers (Membership) Privileges Settings

There are different category of members such as faculty, guest faculty, research scholars, postgraduate students and other members. Not all the categories may have similar type of borrowing facility. For instance the faculty can get the book issued for one semester and the postgraduate and research scholars will be given a period of 15 days for holding a book. Similarly, the patrons borrowing facilities may vary regarding the number of books issued to them. Post graduate students can borrow four books, research scholar 5 books, whereas faculty members borrow up to 15 books other than their project books. Libraries are containing different type of material such as - monographs, serials, these, dissertations, project reports, reference books, textbooks and magazines. Not all the types of material can be issued as per the library policy – such as serials, bound volumes, expensive reference material and magazines. So depending upon the borrowing facilities of each category of patrons and the type of material the system parameters need to be set at the time of initiating the circulation operations through ILS software. The table 4.2 indicates a sample matrix that defines borrowing privileges based on the type of patron, material with the details of loan period and lead time etc.

4.3.3. Transactions

Each of the circulation transactions generate a record consisting of mainly the transaction ID, patron ID with the respective dates. The figure 4.3 reflects the data structure of a transaction record file.

Table 4.2. Membership Privileges Matrix of a University Library

User category	*Borrowing Limit As per the type of material*					*Loan Period Limit (incl. Maximum renewals)*				*Fines for late per day*			
	No of cards	*M**	*S*	*TH*	*AV*	*M*	*S*	*TH*	*AV*	*M*	*S*	*TH*	*AV*
Faculty	15	10	2	1	2	60	6	2	1	0	0	0	0
Research Scholars	5	5	0	1	0	21	0	2	0	0.5	0	0.75	0
Post Graduate students	4	4	0	0	0	21	0	0	0	0.5	0	0	0
Under graduate	4	4	0	0	0	21	0	0	0	0.5	0	0	0
Adminis-trative staff	2	2	0	0	0	21	0	0	0	0.5	0	0	0

(* M - Monographs; S-Serials; TH-Theses; AV- Audio Visual Materials)

TRANSACTION _ID. : This is automatic based on the particular transaction
USER_ BARCODE. In this the user is identified who is involved in the transaction
HOLD_ID. Refers to the user who is physically present in the transaction
DATE_LOANED.
DATE_DUE.
DATE _RETURNED.
DATE_RECALLED.
DATE_REPORTED _LOST.
DATE_FINE_CALCULATED.
FINE_AMOUNT.
ACTUAL _FINE_COLLECTED.
BALANCE_DUE.
RENEWAL_COUNT. Total number of times renewed.

(Haravu, L.J. 2004)

Fig. 4.3. Data Structures of a Transactions Record

4.3.4. Transactions Using Barcode Equipment:

The items in the library need to be barcoded with the accession number or call number before releasing to stacks and circulation. A barcode label is pasted at specified location of the items at the time of acquisition and technical processing. Similarly, the library members are provided with photo identity cards with their unique number or other alphanumeric code assigned to each of them, as a barcode. The barcode standard that is commonly followed in libraries is Code 39 also called the 3 of 9 Standard. It allows alphanumeric symbols to be used in the barcode and is therefore well suited to libraries. Many organizations issue employee identity cards with unique ID and the same card could be used by the library as patron ID cards for circulation transactions, as long as a unique barcode is assigned to each employee/student and made available on the ID card. It is used as multipurpose card in many University Libraries.

A barcode reader uses a photo sensor to convert the barcode into an electrical signal as it moves across a barcode. The scanner then measures the relative widths of the bars and spaces, translates the different patterns back into regular characters, and sends them on to a computer or portable terminal.

Every barcode begins with a special start character and ends with a special stop character. These codes help the reader to detect the barcode and figure out whether it is being scanned forward or backward.

Barcode equipment require high quality labels, otherwise defects in printing lead to wrong reading of data. It is of utmost importance that barcode labels have high contrast. For this usually polyester labels are used, which is free from imperfections and give good contrast and also durable.

Barcode Label **Barcode Scanner**

It helps in quickly capturing and reading the data while issue and return of books.

4.4. SUBSYSTEMS OF CIRCULATION SYSTEM

4.4.1. Registration of Patrons

The initial operation of circulation module is building patron database by registering patrons. The patron registration will be done at the time of their joining the University. Normally the Institution issue a multipurpose identity card which serves as membership card. It contains important data elements such as name, address, department, email id, phone/mobile number of the patron in a prescribed format against their application. The patron work form exists wherein in the beginning itself these field are entered. The email address helps to send reminder to the defaulting members. The type and category of books that can be borrowed is set in the membership matrix.

This system should be capable of a adding a new record and deleting a record when the course is over and in between if the student leaves the institution. Some mandatory fields are required to be filled without which patron record cannot be created. It should be possible to edit, modify and update a patron record. Tracking the membership record for knowing particular type of information about the patron. For handling other subsystems operations like charging and discharging transactions, the system needs to access the patron database. Since the transactions involve the safety and security of library collection, it should only allow authorised staff members for adding, editing, modifying and deleting data from the patron records.

4.4.2. Issues Sub-system (Charging the transactions)

To issue the reading material to the authorized users of the library. The aim of the subsystem is to quickly and efficiently issue the documents without waiting for a longer time at the circulation desk. Presently the circulation module is integrated with advanced security systems such as RFID, allowing even self – checkout and drop- box for check-in operations. The multipurpose card issued to the patrons containing a unique barcode I.D, and when the barcode scanner verifies the authenticity of the user he will be allowed to borrow depending upon their borrowing privileges. They are allowed to borrow multiple items at a time without rescanning the user ID again and again.

The system should alert the staff if a book is reserved so that and also control the issue of book reserved item book on different user. The system also will not allow a non-circulated items such as reference books, theses & dissertations and journal issues, back volumes. This system does not permit an issued book a another borrower. Such controls, precautions, alerts and preventions while issuing helps in effective and accurate issue transactions.

4.4.3. Return of books

This subsystem helps to return the borrowed materials by cancelling the charged item against their account. In this system the borrower need not be physically present to return the books, but only the item that is borrowed needs to be presented at check-in counter or drop-in box. This subsystem allows return of the book immediately updated in the pattern transaction. It should also prevent unsuccessful return of the item by alerting the staff that the item has not been charged at all. When the item is returned and if there is reservation for the same item there should be alert message prompting the staff member to reserve the item. Such reservations is done automatically invoking the user id who has reserved the item and he will be informed about the availability of the item in the library. Receipts should be generated for the items returned either by itself or on demand.

4.4.4. Renewals Subsystem

This enables the borrower to renew the items that are already charged. The system should permit online renewal of the item without visiting the library. Default renewals should be allowed according to the privileges recorded as per the type of document and user in the matrix. The system also prevents renewal of reserved items.

4.4.5. Reservations Subsystem

This subsystem is available for the use of both library staff and users. In a networking system the user should be able to reserve the required item from his own terminal if it was issued to another patron. Such a facility is available through recent OPACs of library automation systems.

- This system may define the privileges to reserve the material and will be able to define the patron's type and document type privileges that are already set in the privileges matrix. All types of patrons may not have same privileges to reserve books.

- So the system will prevent the restricted patrons to reserve any material and also restricted types of material to any patron. If a borrower is placing a reserve for a document that he is not supposed to borrow the system will not allow him to do so by alerting a message.
- When a borrower is placing reservation for a document he should do so by using a title and not place hold on a specific copy. The library staff can place a hold on the same specific copy. These two types of reservations should be possible.
- When more than one patron places a hold on a title the subsystem should create a queue of such reservations. The upper limit of reservations can also be set in the privileges matrix and if the upper limit has been reached then the system should alert the user not to place the reservation.
- This subsystem should also send appropriate messages to the user who is first in the reservation list when such an item is being returned by the return subsystem. The reservation queue should push up the queue when the reserved item is charged to the first reserved user who was the first person in the queue to borrow.
- Only authorized staff will be able to modify the reservation queue for the item.
- Users can reserve the item via the OPAC and they should also be able to cancel the item for which they reserved earlier.

4.4.6. Recall subsystem

This subsystem should be able to recall the borrowed items before the due date in case of academic activities such as to place the book in the reservation in the beginning of the semester or while stock inventory during summer vacation. This subsystem should send recall notices either in printed or electronic form. When the user logs in to the system via the OPAC he should be alerted with the message that the item which is issued to him is being recalled for academic purposes.

4.4.7. Overdue subsystem

This subsystem should be able to generate claim notices for all the materials by due date or the user. This subsystem should produce overdue lists for all those habitual defaulters who have been and holding items for a longer period of time than allowed. This subsystem should generate no-dues certificate for the patrons who have completed their studies and those who are leaving the organization. While doing so the subsystem should update the membership record indicating the expiry of the membership of the candidate to whom the no dues certificate has been issued.

4.4.8. Fine (Overdue charges) Subsystem

This subsystem should calculate fines for the defaulters who do not return the book on the due date. It should calculate the fines automatically based on the data of privileges in put in matrix. The data defines the fine structure as per the type of user and document. Then it should be able to fix upper limit for fine amounts for each user and document type. It should permit partial payment of fines in deserving cases. Receipts should be generated for fine collection. It should allow forwarding the amount collected for overdue charges to the accounting department of the organization. Further it should be able to maintain a chronological statement of collections as per user with the details of patron ID and amount collected.

4.4.9. Inter Library Loan (ILL)

The request for an item is received from the user through OPAC and the library sends the request to other library which has that particular item. As soon as the item is received on loan and the user who has requested the book will be intimated and loaned to him. After the book is returned to the library the loan record should retrieve the loan record from the library from which it was borrowed and return it to them. Similarly when other libraries request for some material the library again maintains a patron record for institutional library and lends the same to the library that requested the item. When it is returned the book is sent to the stack area and the status of the book is updated. The library should maintain a transaction history of inter library loan accounts for statistical purpose and also audit.

Now days a part of consortia the INFLIBNET program is providing Document delivery services through J-Gate@UGC INFONET program. They have identified 26 document delivery centres for delivering articles to other libraries. This portal allows consortia members to access articles available by clicking the full text or else they can request for the item through this portal. When request is made the second window takes to the library which has the item and the request is made. Through J-gate portal photocopies of journal articles can be requested by the faculty and research scholars from any member university directly without depending on library at free of cost. The DDS process is diagrammatically presented in the following screenshots. Authorized users (within recognized IP range/environment/ campus) will be able to put their query through quick, advanced search interface or by browsing through journals list, selecting volume/number, table of content and finally the article by its location or locations. Further, users will be able to register for their favourite journals and get their alerts notified through registered email .The requester should provide phone number and I.D number so that when the library receives the request the user can be intimated to collect the copy. Figure 4.4 to 4.7 indicate the online document delivery process among institutional users.

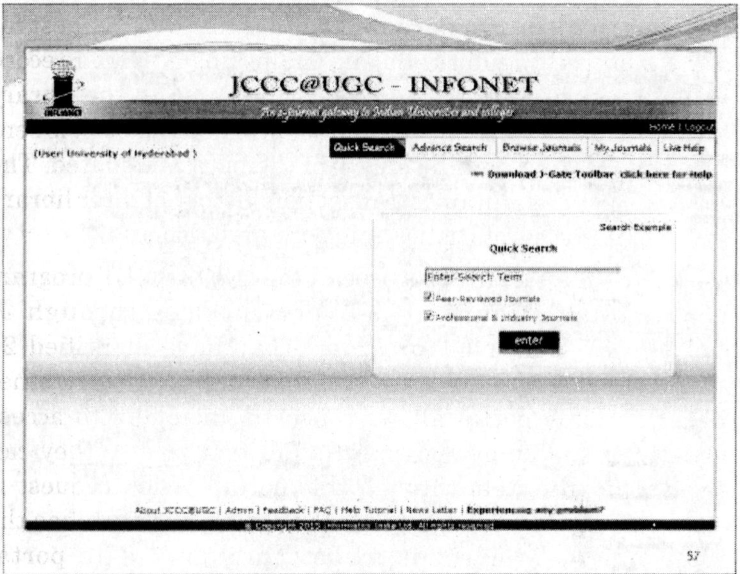
JCCC@UGC - INFONET
Home | Logout
(User: University of Hyderabad)
Quick Search
Advance Search
Browse Journals
My Journals
Live Help
Download J-Gate Toolbar click here for Help
Search Example
Quick Search
Enter Search Term
Peer-Reviewed Journals
Professional & Industry Journals
enter
About JCCC@UGC | Admin | Feedback | FAQ | Help Tutorial | News Letter | Experiencing any problem?
57

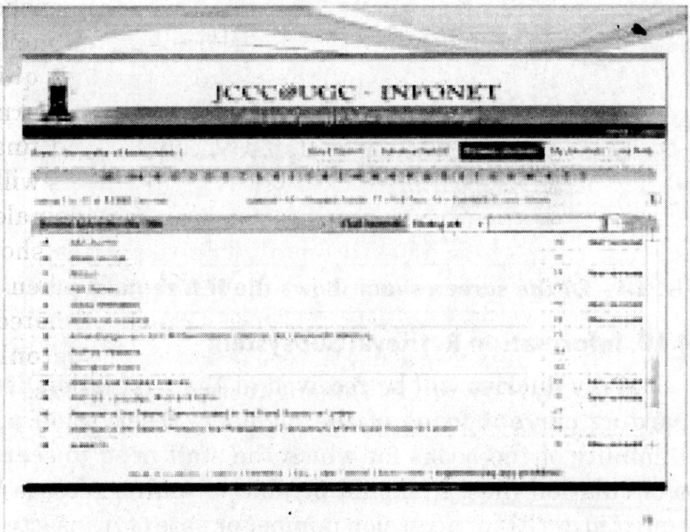
JCCC@UGC - INFONET

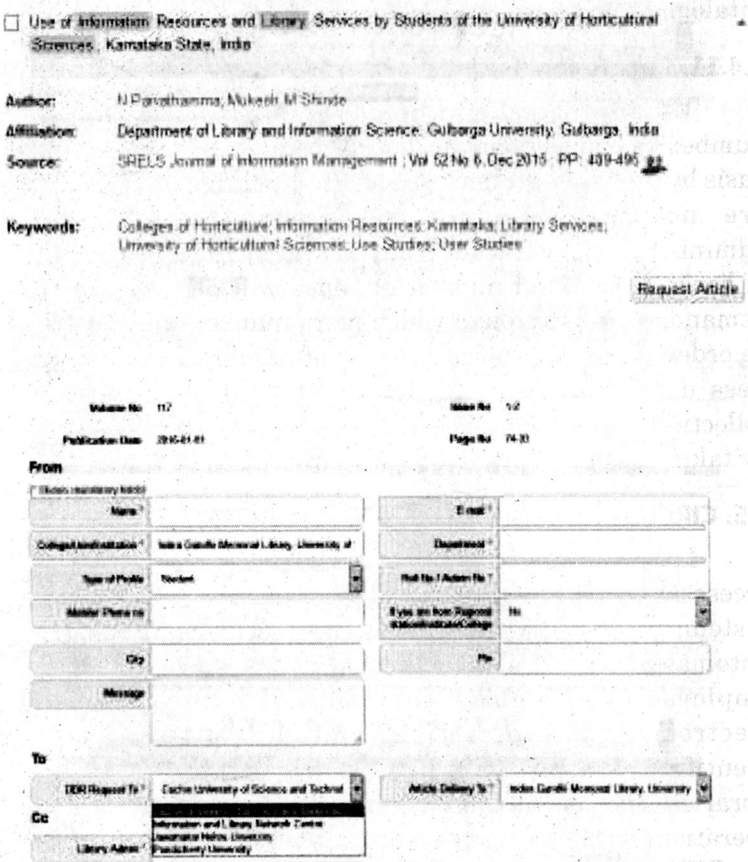

Fig. 4.4 - 4.7 the screen shots shows the ILL request process

4.4.10. Information Retrieval Subsystem

Many queries will be received at the circulation desk regarding current loans of the member, reservation and availability of the books for which the staff need to search the circulation files. It should be able to search records by member id or title or accession number or date of transaction. To search reservation data from the reservation files to know the status of the specific item. Search the transaction of data to know the information items on loan. Search the online catalogue to retrieve the books data.

4.4.11. Circulation Statistics

Usually the statistics need to be maintained regarding number of transactions on hourly basis, daily or monthly basis by types of user and type of document. These statistics are normally required to present before audit, administration, by tracking the reservation file and numbers of books issued and number of times will give the highly demanded books through which more number of copies can be ordered or some copies can be shifted to reserve section. Less used books can be thought of shifting to passive collection or weed out to create more space for the new books by taking approval of the library committee.

4.5. CIRCULATION OF BOOKS AND SECURITY

Loss of books is a major threat to libraries in open access system. The conventional methods like closed access system, security cases to protect CDs, security guards and automatic communication links with police are however employed to safe guard the material from theft. The electromagnetic detection and Radio Frequency Identification (RFID) are being employed in the modern libraries in recent decades. When automation of in house operations are done the software should be compliant with the RFID security system so that the library materials are not only protected from theft but it enhances the speed in transactions and proves to be more user centric thus providing modern services to the user like self- check in & check out and no queueing or waiting time.

4.6. SHARING OF DATA WITH OTHER SUB SYSTEMS

Whenever issue and return transactions are done it calls the bibliographic data from the library database. To know the reservation and loan status it accesses the user files to know how many reservations are done and for how many books.

Users query through OPAC to know the status of the books and loan items against them. Users can via OPAC send their request for acquisition of new books. Send their requests for Inter library loan.

5

Automation of Serial Control and Holdings

5.1. INTRODUCTION

Periodical is a publication of which each volume has independent contributions, not forming a continuous exposition, usually by many personal authors and the contributions in successive volumes also being, in general, different, but all the subjects falling within one and the same region of knowledge, contemplated to be brought within its purview. Harrods's Glossary defines serial as "any publication issued in successive parts, appearing at intervals usually regular ones and as a rule intended to be continued indefinitely. The term includes periodicals, newspapers, and annuals, numbered monograph series and the proceeding transactions and memoirs of societies. (1987). S.R. Ranganathan (1958) in his Classified Catalogue Code defined periodical as "a publication of which each volume is made up of distinct and independent contributions, not forming a continuous exposition, normally by two or more personal authors and normally the specific subjects and the authors of the contributions in successive volumes."

— Journal and serials are synonyms to periodicals.

Periodical was the preferred term earlier. Now due to advent of electronic media the preferred terms are electronic journals and online journals.Fastest medium of communication of the current research findings.

— Enormous literature is published through serials.

— Report primary data and publish articles, book reviews, advertisements, announcements, current events.

— Publishing from scientific societies, research organizations, academic institutions, commercial publishers, government and non-government organizations.

— Applying the latest techniques of Communication, Science & Technology in formatting and distributing the Content.

— Publication issued in successive parts. Continued indefinitely with specific periodicity at regular intervals.

The serials bibliographic record is similar to books or any other library material, but the format varies because of its distinct characteristics. Moreover, it is usually accompanied by the holdings record associated to each specific location. The acquisition operations, technical processing and circulation of serial issues/volumes are following more or less similar work flow with some variation.

5.2. SPECIAL CHARACTERISTICS OF SERIALS

Each serial is unique in its Characteristics: Content, Treatment, Frequency, Publication Format, Schedule, and Distribution. It appears with Numerical and Chronological designations. Many software vendors still lack certain functionalities with regard to serials control and acquisition module.

- The serials are published by several publishers who publish in different frequencies for which the library does not have any control over such scheduling pattern.
- A serial could be published either daily, weekly,

biweekly, fortnightly, quarterly, monthly, nine times a year etc.Some of the serials are issued irregularly without knowing how many issues will be published in a year and when the next issue is due. Some serials are scheduled according to seasons such as autumn, spring, summer, winter.

- Suddenly the frequency may even change. Numbering of each volume varies. The serials number is done with the beginning of number one of each volume. There are also serials which are numbered continuously. Some use roman numerals for numbering their issues.
- Certain issues of serials may suddenly decide to publish as a combined one, for e.g. a serial that is published quarterly may think of combining the publication of two successive issues under one cover.
- Occasionally a special issue focusing on a particular topic might be scheduled over and above the other issues in a volume. They are included in the annual subscription but usually priced separately.
- Title changes are frequent and unforeseen in case of serials the information normally is given at the end of the volume with the old title and the publisher's communications regarding the changes are uncertain. There are also cases wherein the publisher may split a serial into two or more serials. This is also done at the end of the volume with the old title. Sometimes a new title will be given to the serial by merging two or more titles into either one of the existing titles or totally a new one.
- A serial is normally planned for a single year but there can be a serial having more than one volume per year. Some publishers publish journal and indexes separately as a supplement or include in the last issue at the end.
- Scheduling the journal issues receipts is difficult due to several complexities in their Publication viz.

Variation in Periodicity, additional issues (both Scheduled and Unscheduled), Supplements, delay in publication, ever changing periodicity, publication / distribution systems.

- Uncertain claiming policies which varies with each publisher.
- Loss of issues in transit, pilferage.
- In the present era almost all the print serials are published online while some are published only in electronic form. The subscription of the online journal is tied to the print one. That is if subscription is made to the print then electronic version is free or at an additional price in case of print + online versions.

5.3. NEED FOR AUTOMATING THE SERIAL CONTROL SYSTEM

Due to above complexities and lack of predictability and irregularities in publication and distribution of journal issues, pricing of serials, Serial control is considered as very difficult area of operations. In addition to that they are to be processed for binding etc. for future use, and also inventories should be maintained for serials such as: catalogues, indexes. So Automation/Computerization should help libraries in overcoming the difficulties coming across the Serials management and handling the process.

- Several acquisition files such as- subscriptions, approvals received, vendor's directory file correspondence, currencies, conversion rates file, accounts, budgets, payments, vouchers and their data elements are similar to that of acquisition section, if handled manually involving lot of repetitive operations and duplication of effort.
- In automation these files are maintained with much efficiency. Especially sending reminders, notices for unsupplied items and tracking them is made quite easy in automation. Financial management, registering of issues without gaps and automatic generation of claims

help the staff to devote on professional activities in automation. Several tasks such as tracking completed volumes of sets, preparing binding lists and adding to the holdings data in automation helps the library to have better control over serials. Immediate tracking of subscriptions, invoices and claims help to maintain effective and efficient serials control systems. Maintaining the correspondence with vendors by tracking subscriptions can be made quick and easy in serial automation.

5.4. SERIALS CONTROL SYSTEM - REQUIREMENTS

Design of module basing on our requirements would be the solution for the utilization software and resolving the issues arising out of the serials complexities.

- Serials are normally subscribed against advance payment and it is the practice everywhere, while some are receiving as complementary.
- The allocation of fund against each department. Acquiring serials within the relevant budget allocation will not be possible as the requirements always exceeds.
- For most of the overseas journals the subscription price + mailing (shipping) charges and currency fluctuations together amounts to an increase of 5-10%, which cause problems for budget projections, journal requirements in libraries.
- Procedure of subscription is through the agents or directly from the publishers. Choosing the right option or set /package prices from the publishers.
- Generation of overdue lists or alert against each vendor
- Calculating the proportionate cost of unsupplied items and claiming refunds from vendors.
- Generating alphabetical list and union holdings list thereby indexing it.
- Producing binding lists, accessioning, cataloguing,

classifying and sending to the stack area.

- Systematic processing of the same through automated system to avoid internal and external audit query.
- Can be searched by title, ISSN, keywords, subject, language, country, and publisher, location, either in OPAC or Internet.
- Monitor the renewals and update holdings (both loose issues and bound volumes).
- System would be able to generate the list of duplicates for Exchange Programs.
- Will be able to maintain the records of payments, expenditure, funds and budget allocation/utilization.
- System should be generating approval forms, orders, serials lists, budget & expenditure statements, accession registers, etc.
- Producing Management Information.
- Preparing the Union catalogues.
- Developing the Articles Database.
- Stock verification.
- Manage to record cancellations, refunds etc.

5.5. FUNCTIONAL FEATURES OF AUTOMATED SERIAL CONTROL SYSTEM

Automated Serial Control System is expected to streamline the manually complex serial control operations more easily, economically and effectively. Further it should be able to overcome the complexities involved in the manual operations.

5.5.1. Access to the external source of information

The serials control systems should have access to the external databases such as publisher's websites, online library catalogues and library networks like OCLC. To get the bibliographical verification of data of new serials that are recommended for purchase. It should also support import of data that is not available using publisher's catalogue for price and ISSN. In automated system if it can access publisher's website or serials union catalogue of library network the verification and import of data could be easily automated. This kind of facility is helpful for maintaining accuracy and uniformity in serial records. But to have access to OCLC records the institution should be a member of that. Otherwise it should be able to download from free sites like Library of Congress.

5.5.2. New Subscriptions / Renewals

- Entry of new title serial details for the first time.
- Recording the various budgets heads, posting sanctioned amounts & modifying.
- Recording advance payments/payments to each vendor/publisher.
- Formatting various texts to enable to standardize correspond to authorities, publishers and vendors.
- Generating approval letters to obtain recommendations for renewing journals for the current year, with a provision to transmit through email.
- Generating purchase orders/renewal orders including a provision to send the same online/email.
- Alerting when funds are exceeded.
- Invoicing and sending bills for payments.
- Updating payment details and generating payment forwarding notices to vendor/ publisher.
- Enable to enter details such as: Frequency, Volume/ Issue No/s; date of 1st Issue and expected date or time to receive the issue to update the system with the prediction patterns of the journals to make claims for missing/overdue issues.
- Enable to enter details such as Subscription/Account number and other Reference Numbers to cite in correspondence, renewals and registering for online access.

5.5.3. Journal Issues Management

- Receiving and registering journal issues including complimentary issues.
- Generating the list of today's arrivals.
- Sending claims for missing/overdue issues.
- Sending orders for the binding units' journal issues.
- Accession them to have record of record of back volumes holdings.
- Print accession register for back/bound volumes of journals.
- Back volumes/loose issues records should be accessible to users.

5.5.4. Circulation and Routing

- Issue & Return.
- Generation of Call letters to the borrower members for overdue issues.
- Maintaining List of over dues by member/title.
- Fixing the priorities for routing the journal issues.
- Configuring the Alert messages according to routing priorities.

5.5.5. Information for Management

- Vendors & publishers directory.
- Journals list by year/alphabetical/ budget head/subject/ country/language.
- vendor/ publisher.
- Updating the serials holdings/ bound volumes list.
- Union catalogue.
- Articles database.
- Stock verification & generation of stock verification report.
- Online journals list with details of web site etc.

5.5.6. Users Queries (Retrieval of Serial Information through OPAC)

Already existing records can be called for renewal of titles. Duplication work can be avoided. The bibliographic information and other details could be shared.

- Availability of a specific journal by title / code / ISSN .
- Availability of a specific Issue of a journal.
- Availability of a specific back volume of journal.
- Journals on a specific subject.
- Availability of the journal volume/issue in other libraries.
- Latest Issue of a specific journal.
- Availability of an article in a specific journal.
- Availability of Articles on a various identified topic/s (CAS service).
- Articles related to the interests of identified members (SDI service).
- Whether a specific journal is available online and the way to access (User id/password etc.).

5.6. SUBSYSTEMS OF AN AUTOMATED SERIALS CONTROL

5.6.1. Serials Master File

It contains data elements like title, volume number, issue number from which the new subscription begins, the period of subscription, mode of delivery, vendor records, payment description, budget, and department that recommended the titles. It contains important data about binding of serial issues, number of loose issues to be bound as physical volume, the nature of binding whether rexene or cardboard binding, spine label to be written, place of spine label to be written. This feature is found in the binding functionality of the serial control system.

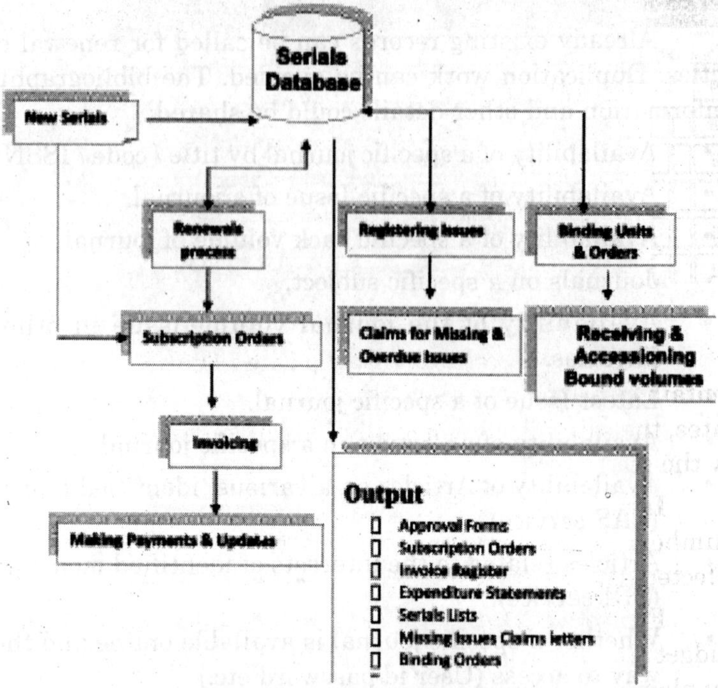

Fig 5.1. Work Flow of Serial Control Module

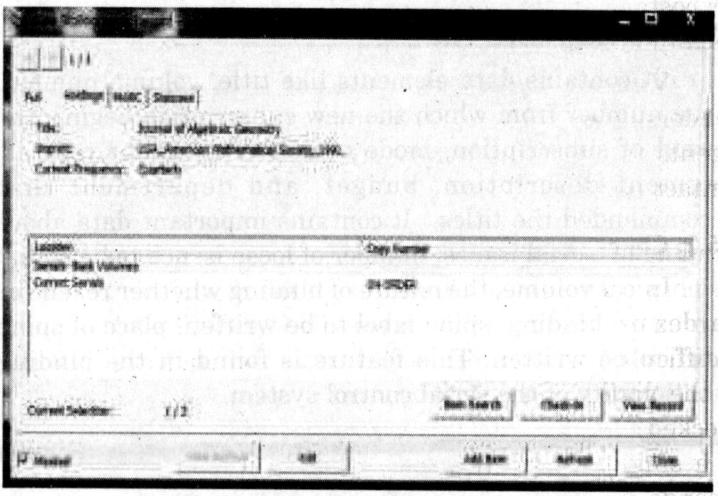

853 tag with quarterly frequency

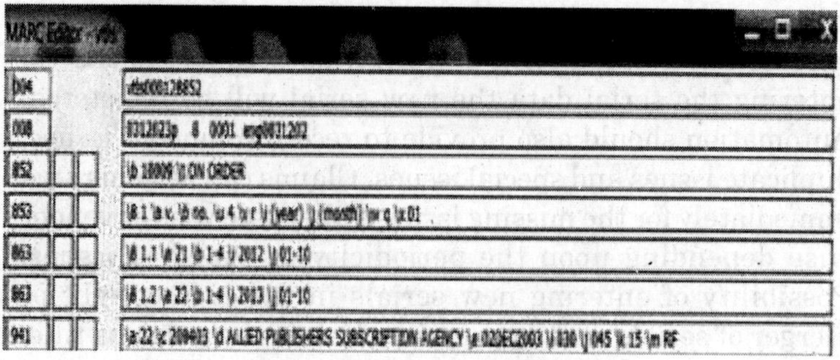

Fig. 5.2. Serials Record

Currency Exchange Rates File : The data elements contain currency exchange control number, RBI conversion rates, the rate of conversion and conversion details modified by the staff member.

Invoice Data File : has information about order number, vendor code, unit price, discount, total funds affected, postage taxes etc.

Financial Data File : It contains information about budget allocation, period of allocation, initial funds allocated, supplementary funds allocated, total amount spent, balance amount available, total amount of discount, amount spent for postage and taxes etc., previous year fund, utilisation of such fund etc.

Vendor Data File : contains information about vendors, their address, phone number, contact persons etc. Agents representing publishers serials, their address and contact number.

5.6.2. Check In Subsystem

In a manual system entering the numerous issues in Kardex or ledger is time consuming and tracking the same is difficult. But in an automated system when the periodicity of the serial is entered the serial can be scheduled and checked in automatically. Number of issues can be entered at a single stroke. Multiple issues can be entered within seconds in single transaction. Prediction of next issue is generated automatically when the newly subscribed serial is received the prediction pattern if entered at the time of entering the serial data the new serial will be registered. Automation should also provide to record combined issues, duplicate issues and special issues. Claims can be generated immediately for the missing issues either title wise or vendor wise depending upon the periodicity or expected issues. Possibility of entering new serials in the case of split or merger of serials with appropriate link to the previous title. Once the correct title is received the checking button immediately registers the issue and it is moved from expected to received status. But if the issue is other than what is expected the library has to check whether the issue is a duplicate or the issue is received because of the reminders sent or if it is delayed publication or the issue is in a changed pattern of frequency and finally if the title itself is changed. The check in subsystem should provide functionalities to address these problems. This subsystem should be able to register special issue, supplement issue and indexes.

For entering serials, in the MARC tag it is necessary to form 853 tag which has following subfield to indicate the enumeration, chronology and publication pattern.

- Subfield for field link and sequence number (generally \81)
- Enumeration details the volume number followed by issue number i.e., v.no.(sub fields a\ v \b no)
- Chronology indicates the year and month ie. \i (year)\j(month)\k(day)
- Publication pattern i.e., \u 4(quarterly)\v r (Numbering recurring code)\w q(frequency)\x 01(calendar change)
- Tag 853 \8 1\a v.\b no.\u 4\v r\i (year)\j (month)\w q\x 01

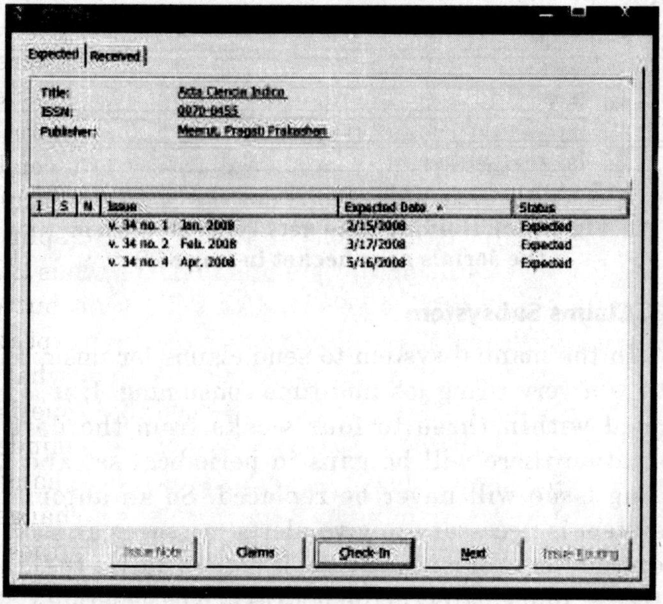

Fig. 5.3 (a). Display of expected issue (monthly frequency)

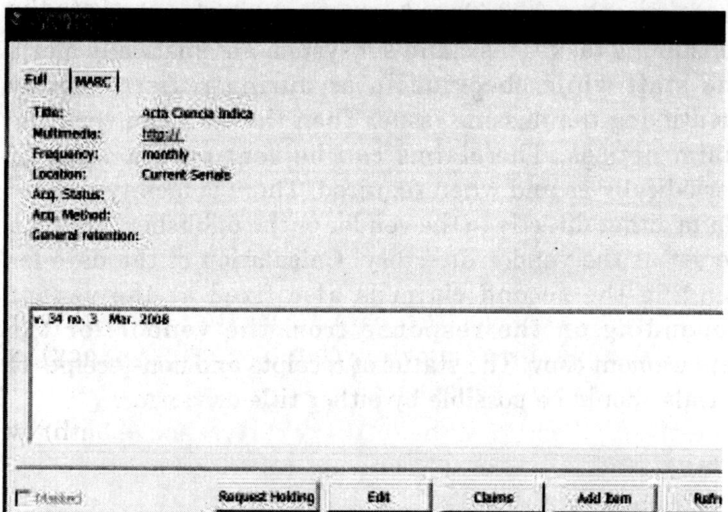

Fig. 5.3 (b). Holdings record with frequency

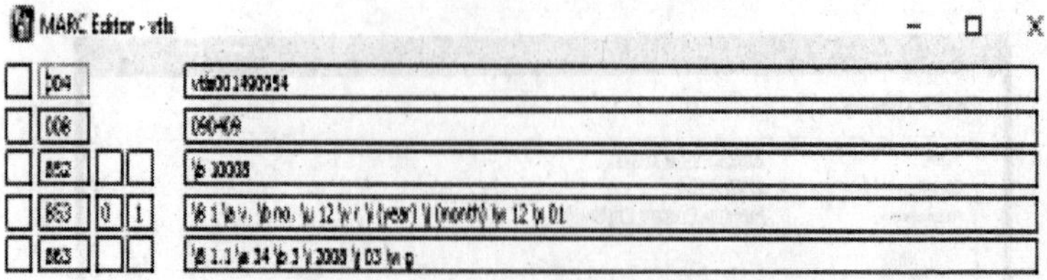

Fig 5.3 (c). Holding data gets generated when the serials are checket in (tag 863)

5.6.3. Claims Subsystem

In the manual system to send claims for unsupplied items is a very tiring job and time consuming. If it is not claimed within three to four weeks from the date of publication there will be gaps in periodical set and the missing issue will never be replaced. So an automated subsystem is necessary to give alerts messages as soon as the overdue issue or missing issue is noticed during the check in process. Immediately claim notices can be generated. The claim notices can be sent once a week and whenever required. In manual system claims have to be tracked by seeing the manual entries and identify the gaps which are very time consuming task. This claim subsystem automatically alerts the staff while checking in or during registration by identifying the missing issue. Then the staff can send the claim notices. The claims can be sent once a week or periodically as and when required. There is facility to send claim either directly to the vendor or the publisher. This can be set at the vendor directory. Calculation of the date for sending the second claim is also fixed at the vendor depending on the response from the vendor for the replacement copy. The status of receipts and non-receipts of serials should be possible by either title or vendor.

5.6.4. Binding subsystem

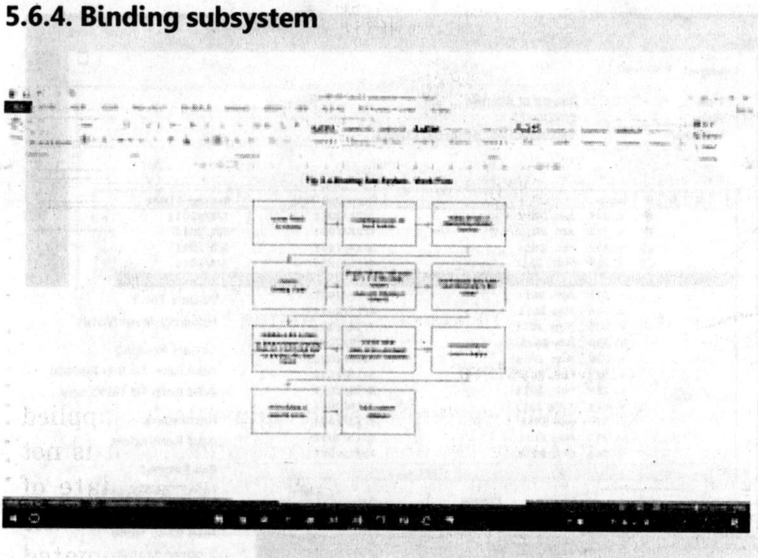

Fig. 5.4. Binding Sub System - Work Flow

There is close integration between the registration of issues and binding subsystem. Some software alerts the staff when the last issue of the volume including the index is received to combine the serial volume ready for binding. Also allow the staff in a batch mode once in a month to collect all the loose issues and to list them and send it for binding. Binding orders are placed from the list of bindery vendors who are included in the vendor directory.

The binding orders should specify different types of binding like rexene, hardbound leather binding etc. Once the binding is completed the volumes are given the status of Bound volumes.

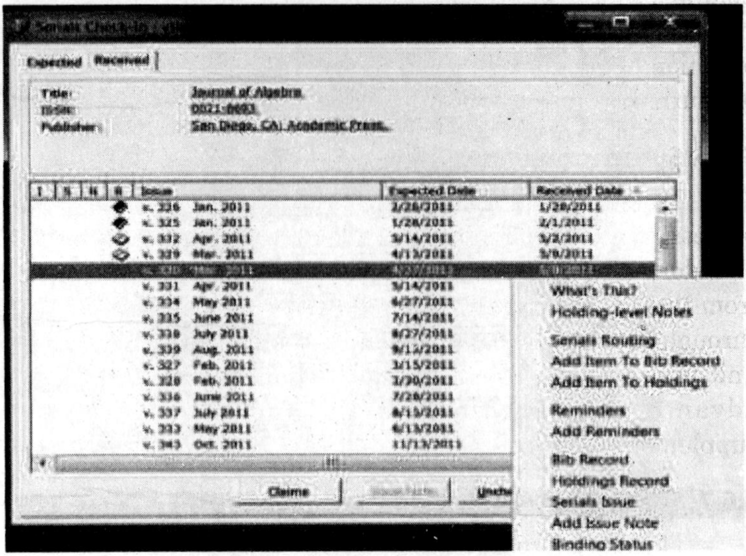

Fig. 5.5. Binding Processes

5.6.5. Union List Subsystem

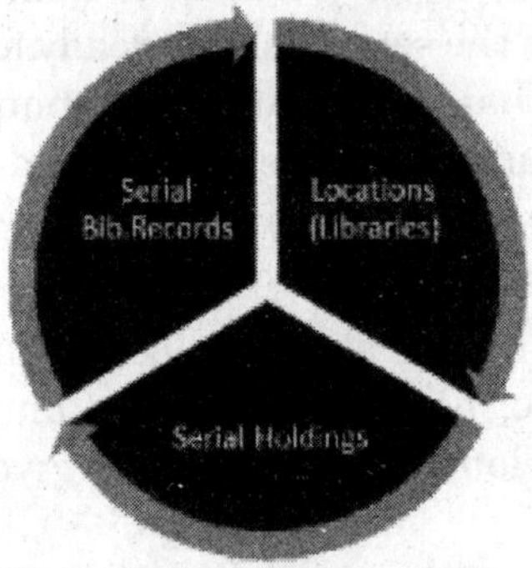

This happens when there is main library with departmental libraries or many cooperating libraries such as number of college libraries. The serial holdings of such libraries will serve as union list of serials and the libraries can share the serial resources. This should be possible by preparing the holdings of libraries by title while displaying holdings in the union list. Retrieve the holdings record by title ISSN or subject keywords. So the principle components of Union catalogues subsystem are – Bibliographic records of Journals, Libraries profile (Locations) and Holdings.

5.6.6. Subscription Subsystem

This helps in processing orders once the approval process is over. Some software's allow electronic transmission of orders. This subsystem should allow renewal of orders from the previous year. It should allow receiving of serials through gift or exchange. The fund account should be handled and invoice processing should be done. It should allow advance payment for serials and adjustment of supplementary invoices.

5.6.7. Search and retrieval subsystem

This subsystem allows the staff to search serials data by different methods. Users will retrieve the serials data through OPAC. Serials files should be retrieved by serials title, ISSN, vendor, subscription expiry date or budget head. The received serials record should be accessible by serial title ISSN or keyword. Serials holding can be searched through the library catalogue with title or ISSN.

5.6.8. Reports Subsystem

Reports can be generated for budget allocation and expenditure. Number of serials checked in and number of claims made should be generated. Reports of advance payment and supplementary adjustment should be generated for audit purposes.

5.6.9. Sharing data with other automation modules

This means that one subsystem should share and exchange the data with other subsystem. The serial subsystem will share the data with catalogue subsystem.

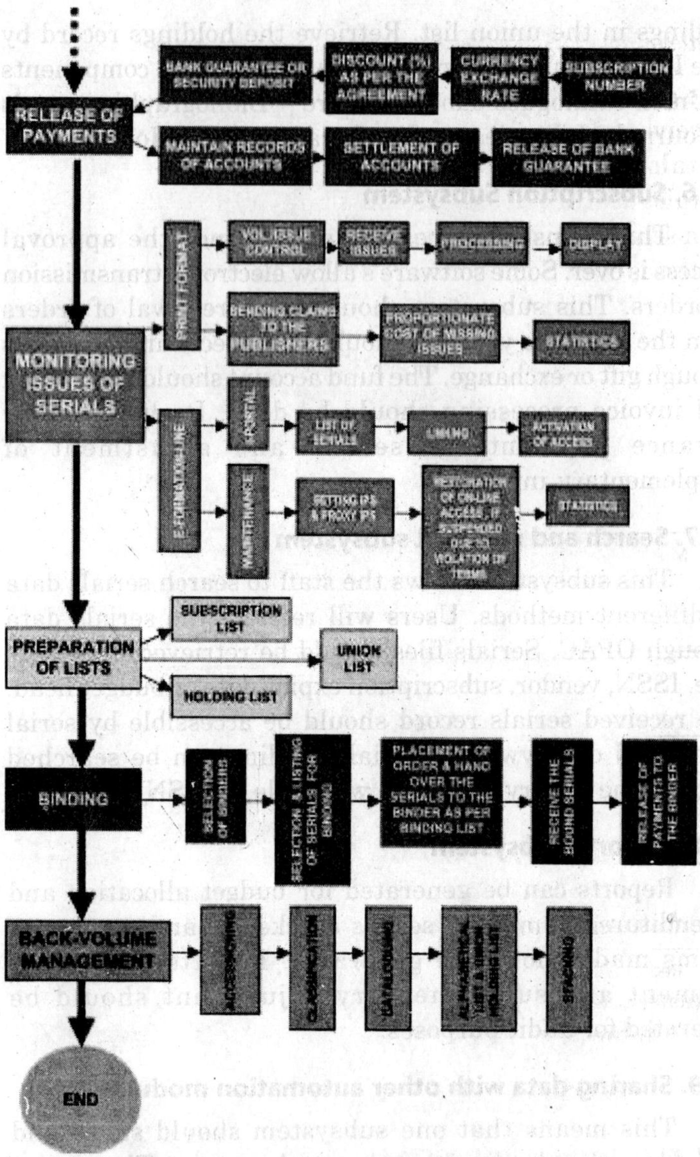

Fig. 5.6. Flow Chart of Serials Process
(www.emeraldinsight.com/0033-0337.htm)

The serial subsystem should retrieve the catalogue record of the serial by downloading the catalogue record into the subscription order record. For instance when a serial is received afresh the serial module should bé able to get the cataloguing data entry so that the new serial can be catalogued. It should be able share with OPAC. The users can search the serials record as well as the catalogue record, of the serials and the union list of serials through the OPAC.

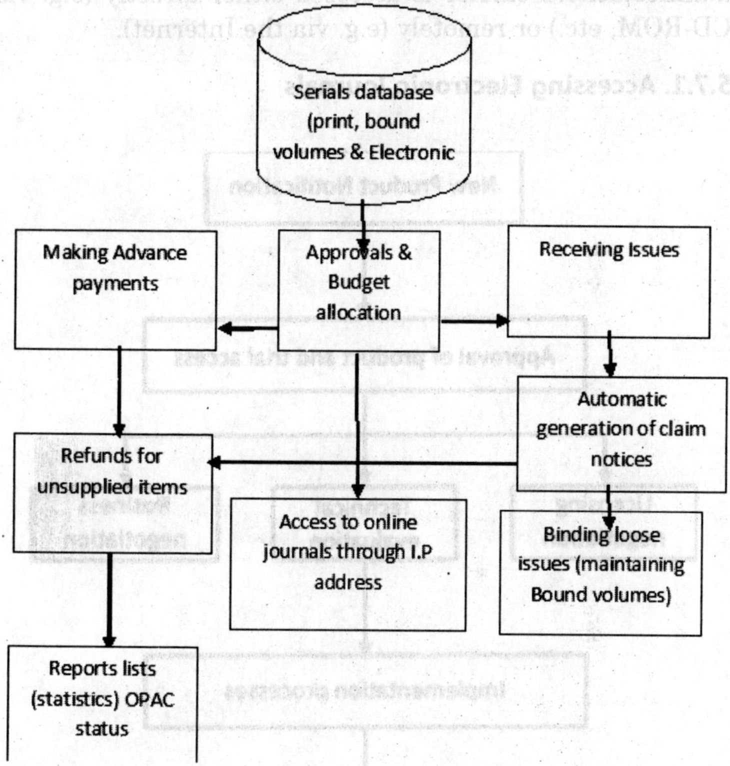

Fig. 5.7. Automated Serials Control System

5.7. ELECTRONIC JOURNALS

Electronic journals can be referred as documents produced, preserved in electronic medium and distributed either offline through disks or online via networks. The terms digital, virtual or paperless or online are used almost synonymously with electronic in spite of some slight variations in them. AACR2 in its revision has included electronic resources and defined as "the material (data and/ or program(s) encoded for manipulation by a computerized device". Library of Congress further clarified that "it is a manifestation of a work that requires the use of a computer for access. Peripheral devices attached to the computer (such as a CD-ROM drive) may also be required. The manifestation's carrier is accessed either directly (e.g. via CD-ROM, etc.) or remotely (e.g. via the Internet).

5.7.1. Accessing Electronic Journals

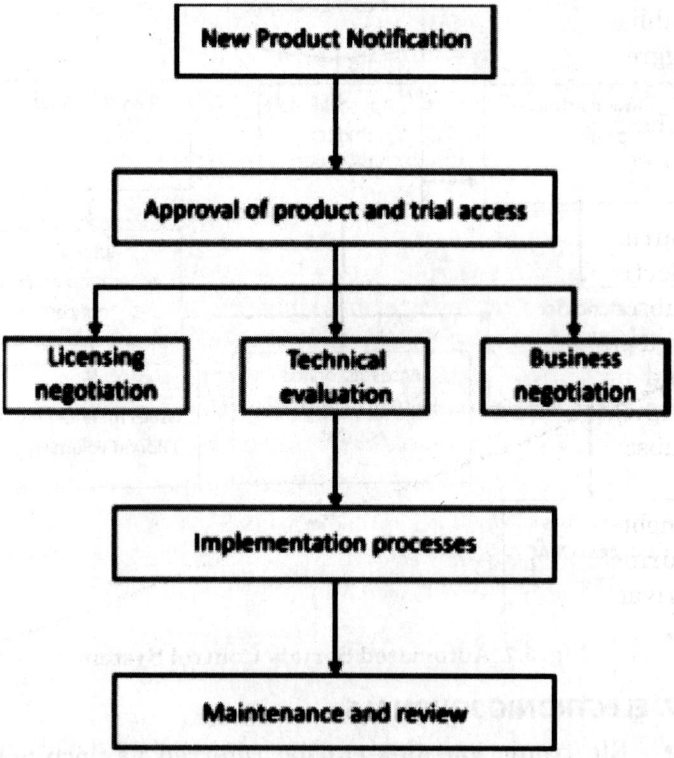

Fig 5.8. DLF (Digital Library Federation) –ERM Flow chart

Academic libraries are pressurized with the burden of maintaining minimum number of journal titles in print and at the same time trying to provide means of access to

Electronic journals without additional or with little financial resources. The birth of internet more and more journals are being published in electronic media thus enabling copyright controls. (Mc Knight1993). With the advent of www there were rapid growth in e-journals because of creativity and productivity has also improved due to network technologies. The advantages of e-journals over print is its easy accessibility, easy to publish, speedy information , low cost and it brings authors and readers close and relieves physical space constrain. Presently every publisher is accepting articles submitted in electronic form for review before publishing in printed journals. Many of the publishers and aggregators are providing online journals plus print journals at an additional cost of 10% to 15%. If print journals are subscribed then online is provided free. The pricing varies for eg electronic only, print + electronic.

Versions are priced together and also collections of e-journals as database packages. Practically selecting an electronic journal refers to five actions. Placing a paid subscription, signing a license agreement, accessing a title on a pay-per use basis, including a title in a library's gopher and providing access through a www site. According to Digital Library federation the process of e-journals subscription takes place in the following manner.

The library's authentication should be efficient, be unobtrusive, require the presentation of credentials only once during a session; however that is defined, protect patron's privacy and be loyal from the vendor's point of view.

- Institutions are provided access based on subscription to print version with additional charge of 5-10 % for online access.
- By user Id and Password.
- Publishers and aggregators provide access based on I.P range of the institution.
- Institutions get the access through being consortia members again via I.P range.

- Referring URL validation.
- By signing the license agreements by the institution if directly subscribed by the institution or through the consortium.
- Open access resources that are available.

The ILS vendors should integrate the management of electronic resources by allowing the patrons to view the license agreements and browser interface to access the electronic resources and view the usage statistics through COUNTER-compliance so that renewals can be based on the usage statistics. The UGC-INFONET Consortium provides E-RAMS (Electronic Resource Management Service) through which member institutions can contact the publishers directly for any complaint and know the status of the complaint. Auto generated usage statistics of the Institution and license agreements are also transparent to the users. The Vendors provide latest technologies such as email alerts and saving them for future reference etc.

Serial module should provide features which are easy for managing and recording print journals, pulling the titles from last year for current approvals and simultaneously provide features for managing electronic/online journals regarding price details, and license agreements transparent to the users and link for accessing the full text.

5.7.2. E-Journals Cataloguing

Catalogue is the basic tool for exploring library resources. Cataloguing practices vary according to their physical format. Apart from conventional print material, the modern libraries need to organize electronic resources receiving through multiple channels for their academic work and research works. The cataloguing practices or decisions vary for e-resources according to the physical format (CD; DVD; Online); type of subscription (Online free with print, single titles, full text databases); acquisition mode (subscription,, one-time payment, open access); type of access (subscription/renewal or open access peer-reviewed or non-refereed free resources).

Regarding the level of searching and indexing, the catalogue options vary.

- Database level
- Individual title level
- Individual article level

Libraries usually prefer to catalogue their own resources especially purchased on perpetual access, but some choose to catalogue all the accessible e-resources for their users.

Customarily, libraries have been adding information about the electronic version to the already created bibliographic record for the print. There is also a cataloguing practice of creating separate entries for print and electronic versions, in specific situations –

- When the length of record with URLs looks complex to the users.
- When the resources changes from print to e-format, especially when print is discontinued and the current availability of resource is only in electronic form.
- If the content of e-resources is almost different from print resource.
- To catalogue exclusive electronic resource database (either full text or abstracts or citations) e.g. EBSCO, Sciencedirect, Web of science, etc.
- When the e-resource contains newer material than the print version.
- When library has no print holdings for the titles.

In addition to the conventional approaches the following descriptive elements are to be catalogued exclusively for e-resources.

- The physical format of the electronic resource (Print or Disk or Online).

- The format of the accompanying material issued with print (disk or online) or with disk (online) or online (with disk).
- Holdings or back files usually offered with the e-resources.
- The special features associated with e-resources.
- Hyperlink/s to the source/s: uniform resource location (URL) with e-resource at specific location.

MARC 21 accommodates the data elements in bibliographic records of electronic resources. It comprises of the appropriate features encoded.

Specific provisions are made available in 006, 007, 008, 856 tags and gets the content of e-resources accessed either from CD Servers, local or publishers server.

Table 5.1. E-Resources: The Significant Fields (Tags)

Tag	*Description*
006	(00-17) alphabet 'm' indicates position for 'computer files/ electronic resources'.
007	(00-13) physical description fixed field. 'c', has special coded information about the physical characteristics of an electronic resource.
008	(00-39) character positions that provide coded information about the record as a whole and the special bibliographic aspects.
022	ISSN for e-resources.
037	Source of Acquisition.
245	Title of E-Resource (Book or Journal or Database).
300	Physical Description.
530	Additional Physical Form Available Note.
650	Subject heading.
856	Up Linking Tag i.e. Electronic Location and Access\u Uniform Resource Identifier.

Electronic journals have become part of library collection and the information need to be provided to users through OPAC enabling their access through hyperlinks. Similarly, it is essential to indicate the availability of online edition with print journal subscription. Furthermore, they need to be identified distinctly and searched to get relevant information.

6

Library Integrated Management Systems : An Overview of Various Software

6.1. INTRODUCTION

The birth of library automation in western countries was seen in 1950s when digital computers became available. In U.S they used punched cards, paper tape, peek-a boo cards and photographic systems. Semi-automatic systems came into force which required human intervention as they were error prone. The automation was first initiated in U.S.A and then in UK due to the availability of good infrastructure facilities in telecommunication and computer technology.

The first housekeeping operations began with the production of catalogue cards in USA followed by the automation of circulation control in large University Libraries. Library of Congress (LC), (USA) developed machine readable cataloguing (MARC) format in 1961.

The MARC was based on three digit number spaces called tags or fields like 100 for author and 245 for title. The place of publication contained three sub fields a ,b, c. The tags and subfields helped computer programs to read and interpret catalogue cards in machine readable storage. The MARC format thus enabled to record full standard bibliographical descriptions based on a cataloguing code such as AACR. The MARC II distribution service began in 1968. BNB and LC began UKMARC project and OCLC (Online Computer Library Centre) in 1967 for resource sharing. Slowly circulation, acquisition, serials operations began in USA using punched cards. In 1990 many libraries provided online catalogues. AACR was revised in 1978 and brought out second edition. In 1980s and 1990s because of library automation and networking, libraries began accessing to outside resources. Since 1990s internet and www had great impact on libraries to operate and serve their clients. MARC 21 was released by Library of Congress in 1999 by harmonizing of U.S Canadian MARC formats and UNIMARC widely used in Europe.

6.2. LIBRARY AUTOMATION IN INDIA WITH APPLICATION SOFTWARE

In 1990s UNESCO developed CDS/ISIS - a bibliographic database management software. dBase and FoxPro database management software were the main products in the use of retrospective conversion of library catalogues. Many libraries began replacing card catalogues with OPACs. The OPAC initiation led many software vendors to develop library automation software using dBase and FoxPro database management systems which most of the libraries were using for catalogues. CATMAN developed by INSDOC, CDS/ISIS by UNESCO, Librarian, Libsys, Maitrayee (developed by DESIDOC) MECsys Nirmals (developed by Nirmal Institute of Computer) Sanjay (developed by DESIDOC under NISSAT project) Tulips and Wilisys along with other software were the first 10 popular library management systems in India in early 90s. As windows and Linux operating systems grew in use many graphical user interface were developed.

6.2.1. KOHA

Koha is an open source integrated library management software, which was developed by Kapito communications in New Zealand in 1999. It was first installed in the year 2000. It has been used in libraries worldwide. It supports multiple languages and following MARC21 format for creating bibliographic records and Z39.50 user interface since the year 2002. Koha 3.0 version has the powerful zebra-indexing engine. Since 2010 it was translated from its original English into other languages such as French, Chinese, and Arabic etc. It is licensed under GNU license. Koha is budget free and maintained by team of software providers and library staff across the world.

The staff and the users can interact easily with the software due to its user friendliness.

Koha was used by Bowen University, OSUN state university library, Salem university library and in many places in Nigeria. Koha meets academic and research public libraries in USA, Middle East Asia, Europe and Africa. Online health facility is available to deal with any problems and issues related to koha usage. Koha version 3.0.1 is used in many libraries.

Koha Features

The koha software has web based OPAC and there is no necessity of installing koha on the user's machine.

- Since it has web based circulation interface and can handle issues, returns and transfers if there is an intranet facility.
- Management of user information. Detailed information about a registered user is made available.
- It allows online renewals returns and reservations which reduces the work at the circulation desk.
- It supports the operations among affiliated libraries, because the software is web based and the user can borrow in one branch and return it in another branch.

- Book reviews and reading history of borrowers: users can review books provide comments, tag them and view their reading history. They can also recommend for new purchases.
- Customized work forms. The work forms can be customized with the basic fields required for data entry.
- Search is also possible with different search fields like author, title, subject and keywords. Advanced search option also exists.
- It is compatible for book acquisitions like placing orders from different vendors maintaining budget and pricing details.
- Serials module helps to catalogue serials and the holding can be viewed via OPAC.
- Virtual shelves: users can have their virtual libraries by keeping specific books to their requirements.
- It supports multilingual OPAC. Patrons can view the records in different languages opted by the library.
- Overdue charges, fines and claim notices- Koha manages to send notices through email to the users. It is compatible with barcode printer and reader. Hence there is less chance of error occurring while reading the books during transaction.
- Security- Koha provides security to authorized users thereby only the registered users can sign in with the username and password to do certain functions on the library database.
- Koha can generate statistical reports: and provide statistics with regard to acquisitions, cataloguing, serials and circulation.

Installation of Koha

The library needs to acquire 17 Pentium IV computers, 18 stabilizers, 18 uninterruptible power supplies (UPS) for the servers. The hardware configuration for Koha installation is Pentium 4, 3 GB RAM, 160 GB HDD, Linux 11.0 operating system and one NIC card.

To install Koha Communities (https://koha-community.org/download-koha/) recommends the following hardware/software

- A Linux server
- Apache
- MySQL (RDBMS)
- Perl
- Root access to the server
- A better level of skill with the command line, Apache, and MySQL tools.

The wireless network option is also employed to provide mobility of use and easy installation. Koha operates usually on the back end RDBMS (MySQL). Larger databases will be running on Oracle. Customization of koha OPAC interface as well as staff or clients and reports module; installation of automatic back up the data entry and the security of library data are depending upon the size of the institutions. Other general features include news label / user card creator, uploading patron images, task scheduler, overdue notices, log viewer SQL builders; and export bibliographic data add value to the library services. Though this software is very useful to staff and patrons, but important challenges with regard to serials is the entering of serial information in the cataloguing module reflects along with other library materials.

Koha Modules

The principle tasks supported by Koha LIS software are – cataloguing, acquisition, circulation, serials and Koha administration. The other tasks involved are Patrons, Reports, Tools, Authorities lists etc. as shown in figure 6.1.

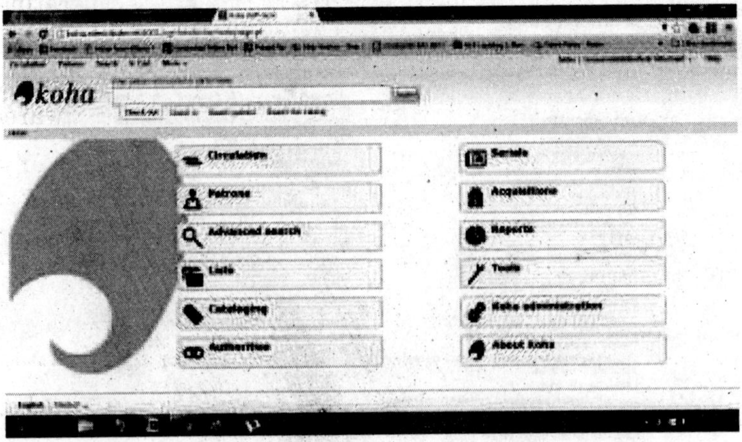

Fig 6.1. Koha LIS Package – Display of Modules

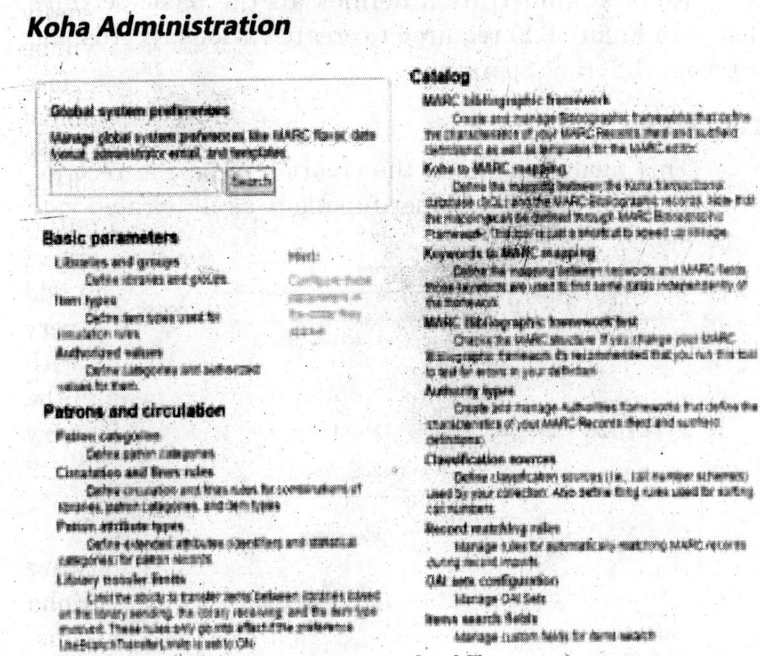

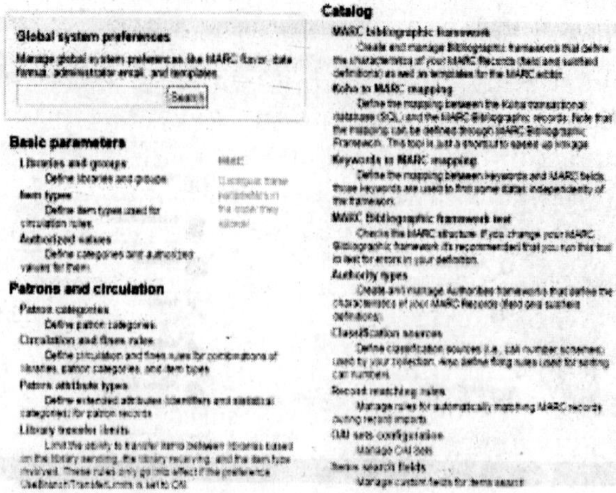

Fig. 6.2. Screen shot of Koha Administration set up

Koha administration defines all the basic settings (listed in Figure 6.2) required to create various records and carryout different operations.

Circulation

This module helps in the creation of patron records, Checkout, Check-in and other functions as illustrated vide figures 6.3

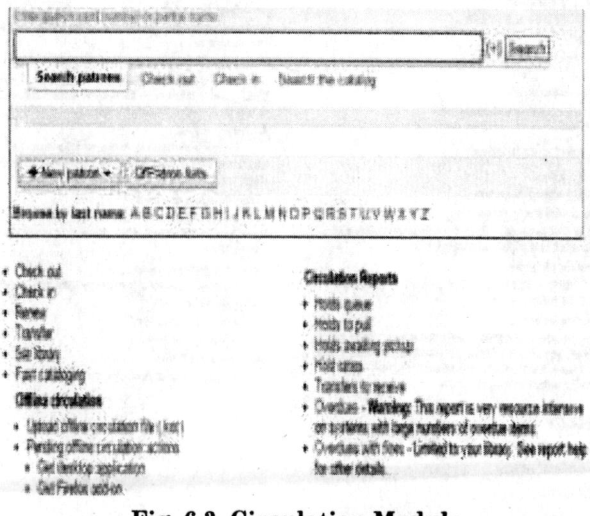

Fig. 6.3. Circulation Module

Cataloguing

Koha Cataloguing module supports the creation, modification and deletion of different types of library material –books and non-book material like Audiocassettes, CD ROMs, DVDs, Videocassettes, online resources in MARC 21 format.

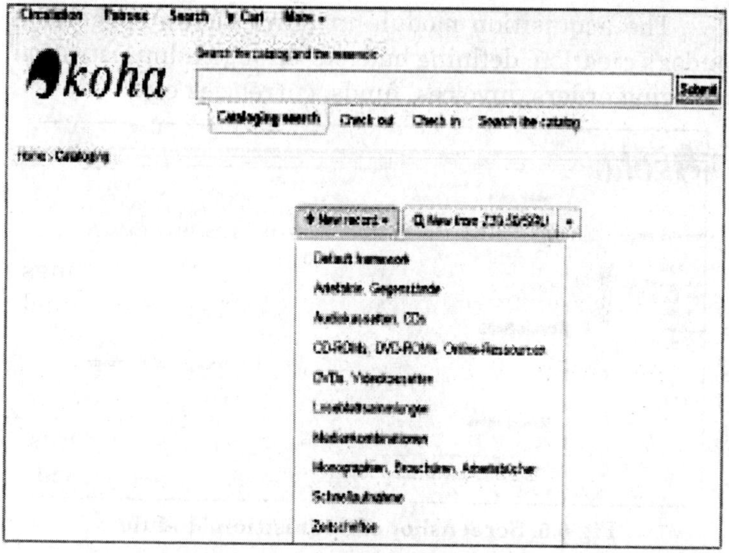

Fig. 6.4. Screenshot of Cataloguing

Serials Control

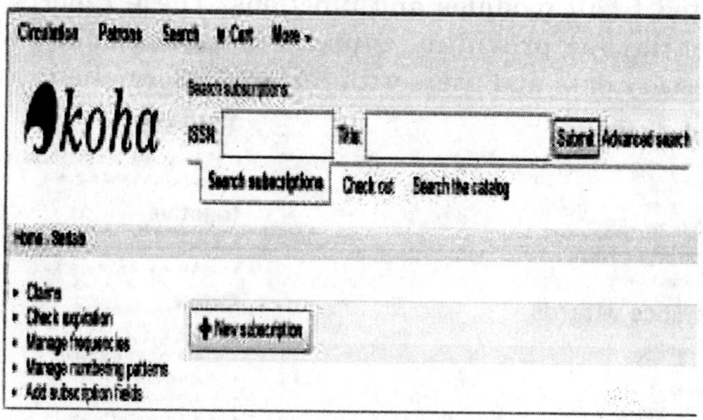

Fig. 6.5. Screenshot of Serial Control

Serials module allows creating new serial records in MARC 21 format and allow retrieving through search interface. Additionally managing frequencies, numbering patterns, claims, subscriptions etc. functions related to serial control that it covers are shown in figure 6.5.

Acquisition Module

The acquisition module in Koha allows suggestion, vendor's creation, defining budgets through administration, managing orders, invoices, funds, currencies etc.

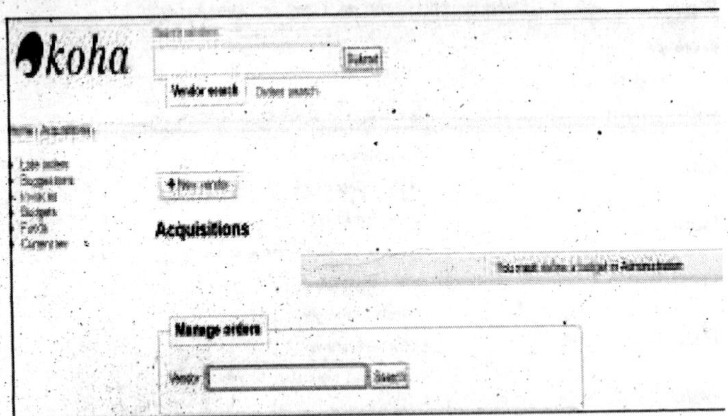

Fig 6.6. Screenshot of Acquisition Module

Koha Reports

Koha enables the generation of following reports related to all modules and functions. These reports are essential for providing support to management with necessary data and users with required information.

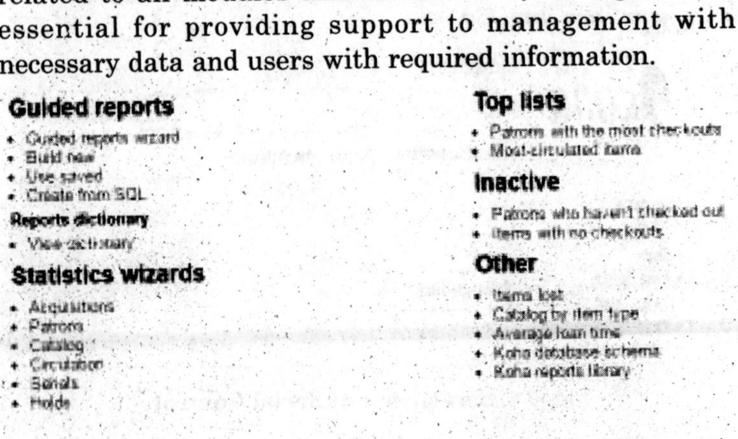

Koha Tools

Koha-tools is a set of programs and scripts integrated with the Koha Library System Software. Koha-Tools is entirely Open Source software released under the GNU GPL Open Source license. These tools/scripts can be downloaded by anyone and use them to customize their library. Kyle Hall, for the Crawford County Federated Library System, wrote these following programs or scripts. (*http://koha-tools.sourceforge.net/*)

Patrons and circulation

Patron lists
Manage lists of patrons.

Comments
Moderate patron comments.

Import patrons
Import patron data

Notices & slips
Define notices (print and email notification messages for overdues, etc.)

Overdue notice/status triggers
Set notice/status triggers for overdue items

Patron card creator
Create printable patron cards

Batch patron deletion/anonymization
Batch delete patrons and delete patron circulation history

Batch patron modification
Modify patrons in batch

Tags
Moderate patron tags

Upload patron images
Upload patron images in a batch or one at a time

Rotating collections
Manage rotating collections

Additional tools

Calendar
Define days when the library is closed

CSV profiles
Manage CSV export profiles

Log viewer
Browse the system logs

News
Write news for the OPAC and staff interfaces

Task scheduler
Schedule tasks to run

Edit quotes for QOTD feature
Quote editor for Quote-of-the-day feature in OPAC

Catalog

Batch item deletion
    Delete a batch of items
Batch item modification
    Modify items in a batch
Batch record deletion
    Delete a batch of records (bibliographic or authority)
Batch record modification
    Modify a batch of records (biblios or authorities)
Export data
    Export bibliographic, holdings, and authority records
Inventory/stocktaking
    Perform inventory (stocktaking) of your catalog
Label creator
    Create printable labels and barcodes from catalog data
Quick spine label creator
    Enter a barcode to generate a printable spine label. For use with dedicated label printers
MARC modification templates
    Manage templates for modifying MARC records during import
Stage MARC records for import
    Stage MARC records into the reservoir.
Staged MARC record management
    Managed staged MARC records, including completing and reversing imports
Upload local cover image
    Utility to upload scanned cover images for display in OPAC

Koha is open source LIS software that has been gaining worldwide popularity and developing with the continuous contributions of Koha community of LIS professionals, Computer professionals and information scientists.

6.2.2. New Genlib

New gen lib was developed by Verus solutions private ltd with the software expertise provided by Kesavan institute of information and knowledge management in Hyderabad in 2005. Since the year 2008 it is available as open source software under GNU (Free Operating System), GPL (General Public License) licensed by Verus solutions. More than 25,000 libraries around the globe are using it. New gen lib 3.0 carbon supports technical processing, circulation, acquisition, serials management, OPAC, administration tasks and utilities on windows. It supports cataloguing of all type of materials and templates are available for different type of materials such as book, serials, thesis, dissertations, journals and newspapers. It has 'quick add' function for having additional tags in the work form in MARC 21 format. Catalogue can be searched with author title, corporate author, call number and any other key words. It has the facility to import bibliographic records into catalogue from Library of Congress OPAC or any other cataloguing using Z39.50 protocol. Once we click the scroll key and choose library of congress OPAC, it immediately opens the OPAC in the new window and we can import the catalogue cards by using basic search, advance search with ISBN or any other key. Then we can save and give the file name as records.mrc and open with note pad with marc format then select all (control +A) and go to new gen lib work form and paste (control +c). Record number will be displayed with status good. Then we can edit and quick add tags if any and save into our database.

Acquisitions and cataloguing

It allows for processing approvals with the entry of minimum bibliographic details choosing budget from the scroll key, which are already created at the time of installation.

- Then number of copies can be added and saved. Catalogue can be searched even for price details and it is editable only at record request details.
- Currency can be entered either in rupee or dollar etc. then vendor can be selected which are already created and available from the vendor directory.
- Then firm orders can be placed with defined order number selecting the title from the database. We can close the current order before which only price can be modified.
- Price is provided only at the order level. Once the order is closed with firm order price details, it cannot be latter modified. Receiving the order by its number and vendor's name and then invoice number and then discount can be entered. Entering of multiple copies is possible in part receipts.
- Claims and reminders can be sent for unsupplied items.

Cancellations are also possible, when the items are not supplied on time.

- Accessioning of received items is possible even when part receipts are executed. To enable the provision, for multiple copies each time the titles are to be entered. Simultaneously entering multiple copies is not possible. Accession number can be deleted and added if mistake occurs.
- From acquisitions to technical processing bibliographic details can be carried forward and additional tags can be added with quick add tag function. Import of Bibliographic records is possible from Library of Congress and other supporting Z39.50 protocols.

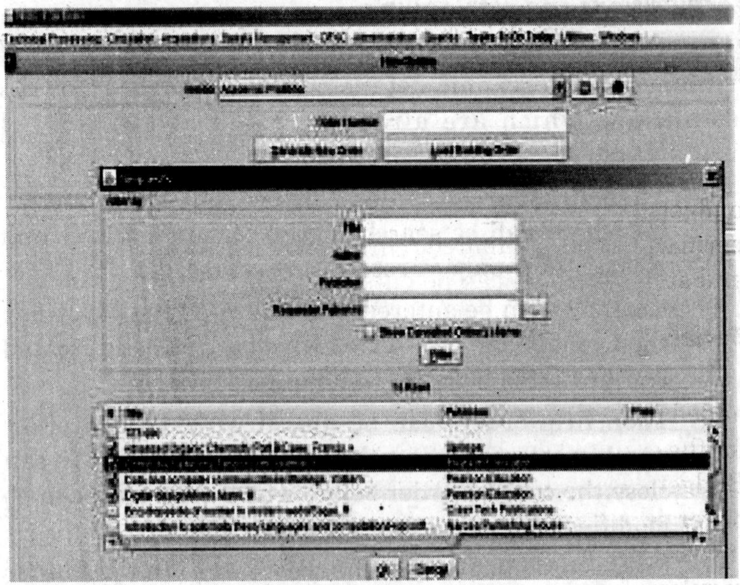

Fig 6.7. Screenshots of Placing Firm Orders in NewGenlib

Circulation

Membership records can be created through administration module for users as well as staff. Issues, returns, reservation and notices to the users can be sent through circulation module. Online issue facility is possible.

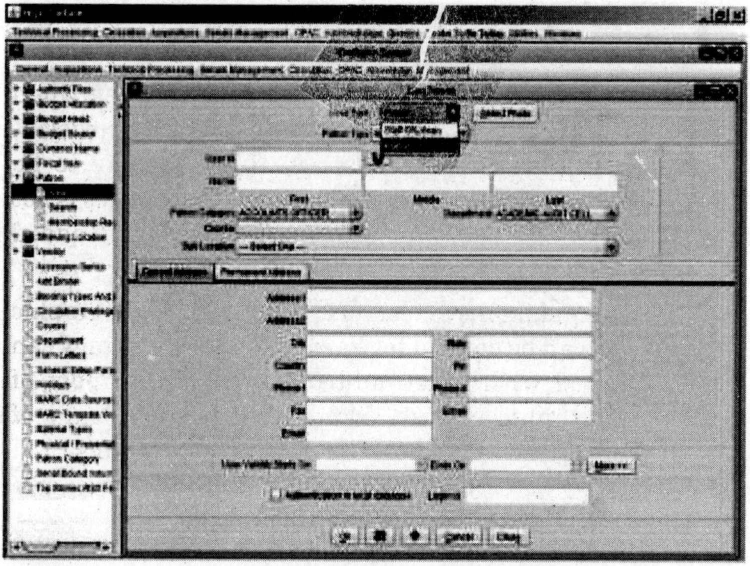

Fig. 6.8. Screenshot of Creating Membership Record in New Genlib

In the administration module, the currency settings, budgets, vendors and user permissions are created. User permissions are unlimited. Through this module new patrons and staff members can be entered.

Serials Management

Through serials management new subscription can be added and also can be retrieved from earlier years to renew for the current year by searching the catalogue for the serials. Budget can be selected to place firm order. Cancellation of order is possible. Original invoices and supplementary invoices can be entered. There is a provision for registering regular issues, indexes, supplements, duplicate issues, out of turn receipts etc. We can add items to the claim queue and issues can be modified.

New Subscriptions or renewals can be done by adding new subscriptions or renewed from the previous year through acquisition module search function by recalling the titles from the database.

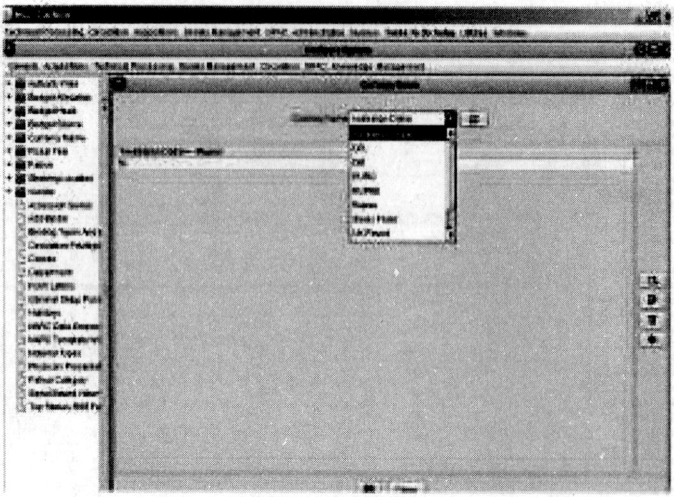

Fig 6.9. Currency settings at the administration module in New Genlib

Binding

The module involves the preparation of issues for physical binding and placing binding order. For this purpose, binding list can be prepared volume wise, and year wise adding the titles with bindery units to binding order. After the binding process the bound volumes can be received, accessioned and binding invoice can be processed.

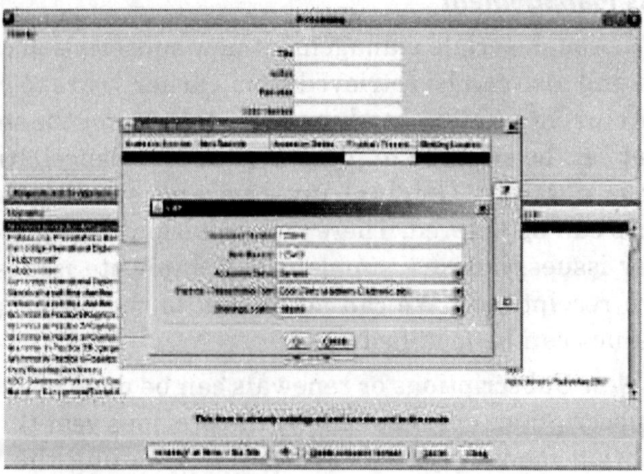

Fig. 6.10. Accessioning of Bound Volumes in New Genlib

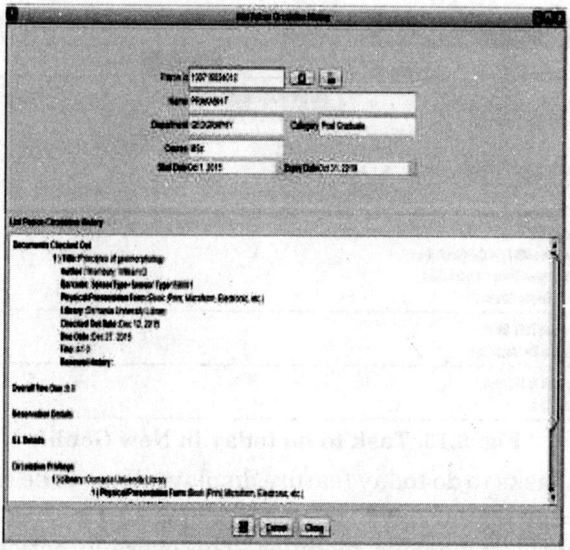

Fig. 6.11. Patron Circulation History in New Genlib

OPAC

Here all types of searches are available i.e. basic, advanced and other searches by type of material. Users can log in and send email recommending for the particular book to be purchased to the librarian.

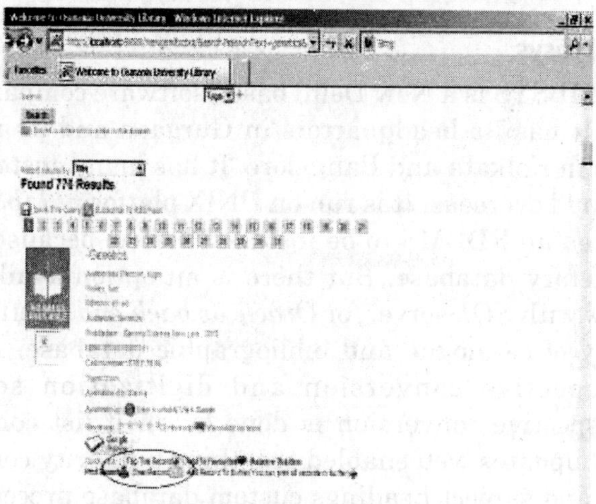

Fig. 6.12. Request for a book purchase through OPAC by Email in New Genlib

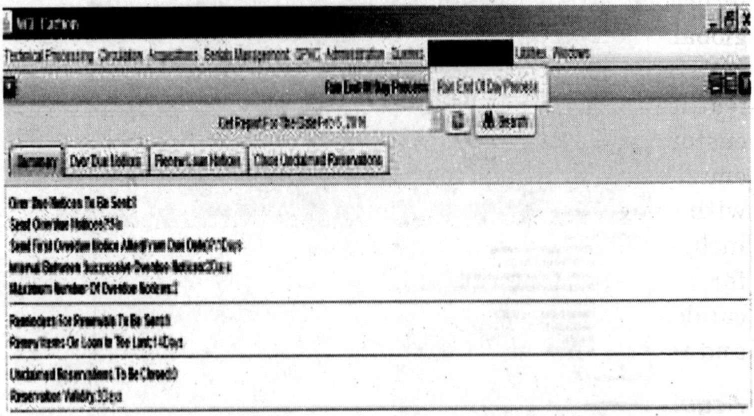

Fig. 6.13. Task to do today in New Genlib

Tasks to do today feature displays items to be executed for the particular day. This feature operates with schedules configured at various modules. The overdue notices to be sent after the due date with a specified interval between due date and notice to be served, successive overdue notices, maximum number of overdue notices, reminders for renewals to be sent, renew items on loan in the last 14 days, unclaimed reservations to be closed, reservation validity etc. All these can be configured and the task to do for the day can be set.

6.2.4. Libsys

LIBSYS is a New Delhi based software company since 1984. It has its headquarters in Gurgaon and its regional offices in Kolkata and Bangalore. It has many customers in India and overseas. It is run on UNIX platform. *LibSys* does not need an RDBMS to be installed before, because it uses proprietary database. But there is an option available for *LibSys* with *SQL* server, or *Oracle as back-end.* It offers high quality of catalogue and bibliographic database. It offers retrospective conversion and digitization services. Retrospective conversion is done by shelf list conversion record updates web enabled searching authority control for name and subject headings custom database processing. It follows MARC 21 format and AACR 2 standards. It has incorporated latest technologies and standards which are globally accepted. Libsys 7 is a product with graphic user interface with multi-tasking support. The most interacting feature in the OPAC. It offers federated searching with customizable look and feel and user interaction through email and SMS.It also provides RSS feeds and integration with google books, book finder etc. interactive features include online reviews ratings, renewals, and reservations for the benefit of the patrons. It supports acquisition cataloguing, circulation, serials, article indexing, web OPAC and reports that are customized.

Acquisition

Centralized purchasing possibility is there when there are multiple libraries located. Order and invoice processing with flexibility for location wise receiving. Online requests for books and approval help in speedy processing of acquisition processes.

Cataloguing

Allows searching of catalogues of other libraries having Z39.50 / OAI-PMH/LIBSYS database. Imported or retrieved MARC 21/MARC-XML records can be edited and downloaded into libsys 7. MARC 21 catalogue interface provides quick online help tips to work with ease.

Circulation

It offers integration of circulation operations with biometric or RFID technologies. Regular reminders can be sent to patrons, patrons can receive SMS, instant alerts and emails. Self-renewals and reservations is possible for the patrons. It supports circulation transactions at multiple locations. It is NCIP (NISO), Z39.50 compliant and hence can be integrated to RFID applications.

Serials

Provides MARC 21 interfaces in all the processes that meet the requirements of online journal subscriptions pattern. Contents page and cover page of physical journal can be scanned and linked to OPAC. Serial module supports obtaining recommendation for renewal updating and for placing renewal orders etc. Serial binding also is equipped with full functionalities ranging from preparing for bindery units to accessioning of bound volumes and bill processing for binders.

Web OPAC

Assist the user in building a search strategy. Based on web 2 technologies pattern gets lots of information through table of contents summary, annotations, author's notes which can be further expanded through search links to Google World Cat, book finder and Google Scholar. LIBSYS 7 encourages patrons to be more interactive through sharing reviews, ratings on titles, emailing or downloading information. LIBSYS has served more than two thousand customers both in India and abroad. 22 years they have been in the field. LIBSYS 7 has gained popularity for refining the work flows and enhanced the library's best practices. At every level it has report functions, modify, quit and process options.

6.2.5. VTLS (Visionary Technology for Library Solutions)

This software supports library operations and digitization. Virtua deals with in house library operations. Virtua supports library automation solutions since 30 years. It supports UNICODE wherein the languages scroll can be used to choose the languages. It also supports RDA (Resource Access Discovery). This software can be operated on both Linux and Windows operating systems. It is based on user licenses. The number of user licenses can be increased by additionally paying for it. Virtua supports all modules acquisition, technical, serials, circulation, article indexing etc. The software comprises of profiler, the administrative module, client, the staff interface, info-station –the web reports module and chamo, the OPAC administrations.

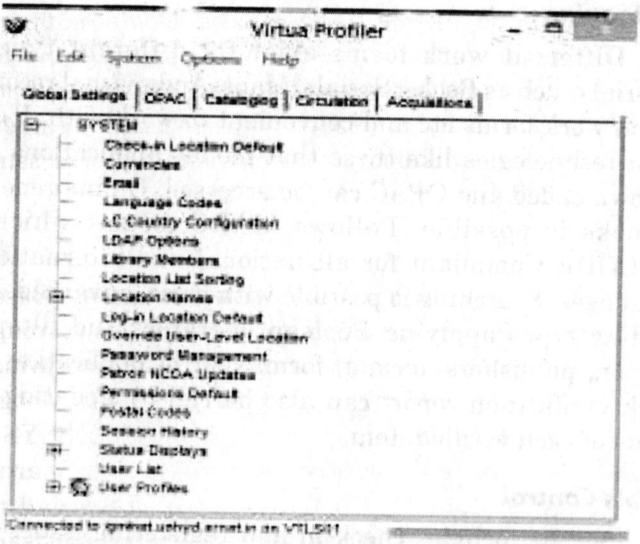

Fig. 6.14. Screen shot of system parameters in virtua profiler

Acquisition

It supports Acquisitions duplicate checking, ordering, receiving and payment updates. The system parameters are set in the virtua system Administration module.i-e the virtua profiler. The currency, budget, fiscal year and user profiles have to be set through the virtua profiler. Permissions for different modules are enabled in the virtue profiler. Library is given the opportunity to choose the base currency during installation of virtua. Once the base currency is set for the system it cannot be changed. The home monetary unit has the exchange value of 1 and other currencies are valued against it by means of a conversion rate. There is tool tip currency converter which can be used, once the exchange rates for each currency is determined in the system.

Gifts books can be entered in the 541 tag, which generates thank you letter as acknowledgment for the gifted books. Acquisition records can be merged into the cataloguing module through merge records in the MARC editor. Minimum acquisition records get merged with the cataloguing work form for entering additional tags

Cataloguing

Different work forms exist for different type of materials such as Books, Serials, Maps, Audiovisual records, patron work forms etc and convenient to work with. It has latest technologies like those that mobile applications can be downloaded and OPAC can be accessed. Online renewal of books is possible. Follows MARC format which is UNICODE Compliant for all national and international Languages. Searching is possible with basic, advanced, and heading types applying Boolean operators and filters – location, publishers, format, form, year of publication etc. Stock verification report can also be run by updating the status of each verified item.

Serials Control

Serials includes check in and registering issues and special issues and also supplements, CD and indexes etc. Processing of serials based on the previous year is not automatically done for ordering. Automatic scheduling of issues, configuring and can be done at the 853 tag applying prediction pattern. When issues arrive check-in can be done with the click of mouse whereby 863 holdings record gets generated. Claims for missing issues and overdue issues can be automatically generated at regular intervals from the scheduling of issues.

Binding

Binding orders can be placed and status of binding can be shown in the system. Loose issues can be combined for binding. If mistakes occur we can manually correct it. Reports can be run only at the info station but not at the module level. The info station has templates in all the modules and reports can be configured. The templates has provision to generate/transmit in html or excel format. Status of binding can be seen in OPAC. Stock verification report can be run at the cataloguing module using the templates. Similarly recently arrived books report can be generated weekly or monthly and linked to OPAC.

Circulation

Supports multipurpose identity cards and borrowers can renew online. Supports barcode and electromagnetic security.. Transaction log can be generated as per borrower, date, year, accession number etc. Hourly transactions can be viewed. It supports membership records, to send reminders for overdue books etc. Patron records can be created with all the details including phone, e-mail & address, department and the type of Patron which enables to transmit necessary mails regarding over dues /fines/ to recall the books reserved by patrons.

Web OPAC

It has basic, advanced and Boolean search options. The Web OPAC 'Chamo' can be enabled in smart phones to have access to OPAC. Search can be refined by location, language, year of publication, subject heading etc. Also by document type such as books, theses, dissertations and serials etc. Users can register from OPAC and view the borrowing status. Location of materials can be stated. OPAC can be used to renew reserve online, to send recommendations for purchase of books and other material.

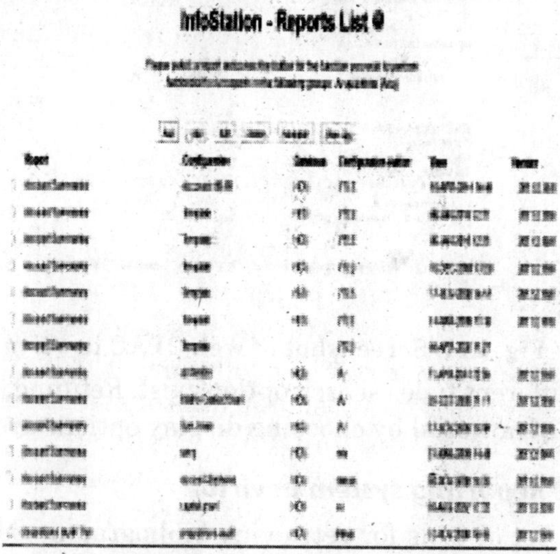

Fig. 6.15. Templates for reports through InfoStation

Fig. 6.16. Screen shot of new books list from Info-Station

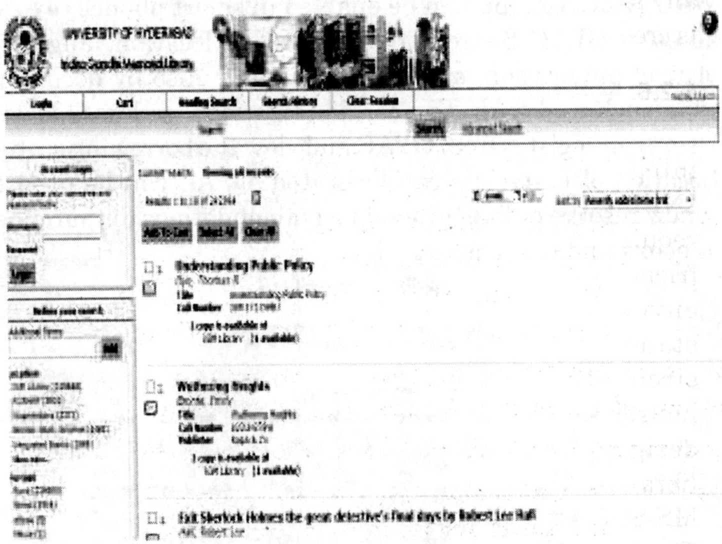

Fig. 6.17. Screenshot of web OPAC in Virtua

Different types search option exist. Refining the search by type of material by choosing display options are possible.

Ad-Hoc Reporting system in virtua

A set of tools for retrieving bibliographic data. Using these tools, one can retrieve any bibliographic tag from the database for use in a report or notice.

The Ad Hoc Reporting system gives the ability to easily create custom reports from the data in the Virtua database. Using this system, library can extract any relevant data from the database for use when it is not covered in the info station templates. The Ad Hoc Reporting system consists of a set of database views that display the data in the form of tables in the Virtua database. Ad Hoc views return normalized data, meaning that fields in the database that contain system codes are replaced by fields that contain meaningful text. The Ad Hoc views can be accessed using the SQL prompt or by using a report-writing tool. Ad Hoc views are available for all sub systems. Stored procedures for creating custom views on the table that stores bibliographic records and display data from any specified bibliographic tag are interesting. After a view is created it can be saved to the system or exported to email.

6.2.6. Software for University Libraries (Soul 2.0)

Software for university libraries Soul 2.0 is an integrated library management software developed by INFLIBNET centre in the year 2000 focusing on the requirement of college and university libraries. It is user friendly software that enables to work under client - server environment. The software adheres to international standards for bibliographic formats, networking and circulation protocols. It is designed to automate all housekeeping operations of the library. Though it was designed for academic libraries, also suitable for other libraries. The database of SOUL 1.0 is designed on capital MS-SQL and it is compatible with MS- Server 7.0 or higher. The database for new version of SOUL is designed with latest versions of MS– SQL and My SQL or any other RDBMS. Soul 2.0 follows Marc 21 bibliographic format, Unicode based universal character sets for multilingual bibliographic records and NCIP 2.0 (National information standards organization) based protocols supporting electronic surveillance and control.

Important features of Soul 2.0

It adheres to international standards such as MARC 21, AACR 2, MARC XML for bibliographic formats. It extends multilingual support for Indian and foreign languages based on Unicode. It follows NCIP 2.0 protocol for RFID and other such applications supporting electronic surveillance and self-check in and check out. Since it provides user friendly interface based on client server architecture and hence in depth training is not required. It is compatible with My SQL, MS-SQL or any other RBDMS supporting multi-platform for bibliographic database. Its special features are cataloguing of electronic resources such as e journals, e books, and virtually any other type of material. It has provision for meeting the requirement of digital library and provides link to full text articles and other digital objects. It provides support for copy cataloguing MARC 21 based bibliographic database. Customized data entry templates for different types of documents are available. Users can generate reports of their choice and format along with template and query parameters. Basic requirements of the library such as stock verification, book bank, vigorous maintenance functions, transaction level enhance security etc are possible and fulfilled in Soul package. Reports generated by users can be saved and sent through email in different formats such as word, pdf, XL, MARC XML etc. OPAC is easy with simple and advanced search. OPAC users can export their search results in pdf, MS XL and MARC XML format. Authority file support facility is available. Data exchange through ISO-2709 standards is supported. An option of Single window operation for all major circulation functions is provided with simple budgeting system. Region wise support is available for help through mails, chat or through telephones which is very attractive feature. Nominal cost with strong institutional support is an added feature.

Acquisition

All the functions like suggestions, order processing,

cancellation and reminders are handled. Receipts, payment and budgetary control are monitored. Master files for currency, vendor and publishers etc along with reports are possible. In Soul 2.0 enhancement updates 7-10 (2.0.0.7.11) issues related to acquisitions with regard to suggestion management, Invoice processing and Title in Process are solved. In Gratis item merge and save issue has been resolved. Gifted by field is added in report listing. Users can attach multiple files in item entry. Facility to generate Accession register. Generation of Barcode of Non–Sequential Accession number is possible with the use of comma separator. In payment register of Acquisition module budget wise reports can be generated.

Cataloguing

This module is used for retrospective conversion of library materials. The staff can process newly acquired resources. It enables staff to create their own easy templates for entering different type of library materials. Users can generate their own customized reports. Authority files database are immediately available for personal, corporate body, subject headings name and series name. Facilitates copy cataloguing in MARC21 format using ISO-2709 standard. Maintains master database of publishers. Entering different languages is possible because of using Unicode character set and creating multilingual database. It is based on MARC 21 bibliographic format. In Updates Soul 2.0 Enhancement 7-10 (2.0.0.7.10) Unicode entry /edit issue was resolved. New feature catalogue card generation is an additional feature made in the cataloguing module. Deleting of bibliographic entry (Administration Module) is made possible. Added help file, screen shots for generating catalogue report, catalogue cards, Server IP settings, Data backup are provided.

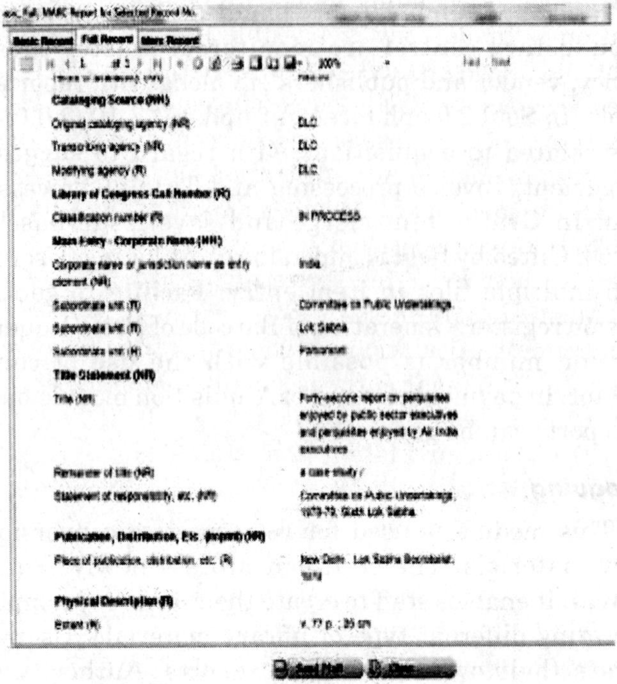

(Source: Inflibnet .ac.in)

Fig. 6.18. Full MARC record in SOUL
(*Source* : Inflibnet.ac.in)

Circulation

All possible operations are taken care in circulation. Membership management, maintenance and status of library items, transaction, ILL, overdue charges, renewals & reminders, search status and report generation showing the status of the items is feasible. The circulation module is fully compatible with the NISO Circulation and Interchange protocol (NCIP) version 2.0 which supports electronic surveillance and RFID based transactions of the library materials. Important features of circulation module are

Membership, Transaction, Inter-Library Loan, Overdue charges, Reminders, Search status, Status of the materials such as binding, lost, replace, missing, withdrawal etc is managed. Depending up on the requirements report generation is made easy & possible. SOUL 2.0 updates brought out several facilities in circulation and other modules. In updates SOUL 2.0 enhancement 5 enabled the Issue & return of loose issues in serial control. Data backup facility was provided in Administration module. In Updates SOUL 2.0 Enhancement 6 Member import utility is merged with SOUL 2.0 applications. In circulation module Serial number, Author, Price fields are included in item status report. Member login in–log report can be generated with hour and minute calculation for whole day. In search by title display of multilingual entry is possible. Member barcode list can be generated. In Updates SOUL 2.0 Enhancement 7-10(2.0.0.7-11) in circulation item status can be changed, Title search, Date format, Member login issue, Validations and Reports are possible. Report generation of No-Due members. Member history and item history report is merged in circulation module. Member code can be copied to member Id if member id is not available during data entry by ticking "Same as Member Code". Editable due date options in transactions menu is provided.

Online Public Access Catalogue (OPAC)

The important features of this module are simple and advanced search facility by keying in the minimum information of the item such as author, title, corporate body, conference name, subject headings, keywords, class number, series name, accession number or combination of any of two or more information regarding the library material. Apart from Simple search, Boolean search and Advanced search. OPAC enables displaying and downloading of records in MS Excel, PDF or MARC XML formats and report the items which are in the Acquisition process.

Administration

When compared SOUL1.0 in SOUL 2.0 some new features have been added. The Module has been sub divided into three major sections for enabling new features. They are User management, System parameters and Masters.

The features include grouping of users based on the policy, transactional permissions over the systems, transaction level security to users. Different configuration settings such as labels, e-mail and other parameters related to the software and common master databases being used in modules.

Fig. 6.19. Advanced Search by title in SOUL

Serials Control

It is based on the manual KARDEX system. The

functions in the module are suggestions, master databases, and subscriptions, check-in of individual issues of journals, payment, reminder, binding and title history. Export and import of record by using ISO-2709 bibliographic exchange format is made possible. Article indexing of journal/book articles. Cataloguing of electronic journals keeping track of the history and changes occurred in journals. Updates in SOUL 2.0 Enhancement 5 made provision for issue and return of loose issues in Serial control. Multilingual title entry is made possible in serial control.

6.2.7. E-Granthalaya: A Digital Agenda for Library Automation and Networking

It is a software designed and distributed by National Informatics Centre,(NIC), Department of Electronics & Information Technology, Ministry of Communications and Information Technology, Government of India. This software supports automation of in-house activities of libraries and provide various online member services.

Installation of eG3.0

e-Granthalaya can be installed by running SQL server 2005 set up from CD on server PC. A client program can be set up from CD on each client PCs, enabling database connectivity from all clients PCs.. e- Granthalaya software is available in NIC server from where it can be installed automatically on the local server and client PC.

System requirements

For client /server mode one server PC with minimum 4GB RAM is required. Windows server 2003/2008/2012(OS) MS SQL server 2005/2008/R2/2012 (standard edition).

Client PCs need Pentium IV with standard configuration of minimum 2GB RAM with LAN connectivity and Windows XP/vista/Windows 7/8. Users of software are Government libraries, (Ministries/departments) Kendriya vidyalayas, Public Libraries, NGO libraries, University libraries, Private Institute libraries, School and college libraries.

Common Features

It supports all modules such as acquisitions, cataloguing, circulation, serials control, web OPAC, Administration module, Micro document Manager, Budgets, search, and web based search module. Retro-conversion is done through cataloguing mode. Since client software is automatically updated data entry program is easier. It is multilingual and UNICODE compliant, supports 10 Indian scripts/15 regional languages. Up to date copy status is maintained. Over internet/intranet member specific data is accessible. MARC 21 format is incorporated and it follows AACR2 for cataloguing. Smart card for member is integrated which is used as multipurpose card.

Members transaction details like dues /fines/ due date are made available over internet/intranet. By one single click CAS/SDI is generated automatically. It is Barcode and smart card compliant and integrated to circulation module. RFID software vendors are working to integrate RFID to e-Granthalaya. Comprehensive library statistics /reports can be generated. Expected loose issues of journals are scheduled automatically. Records editing is possible and there is no locking of records.

From every angle transactions can be searched. It provides integration of e- mail facility. Barcode labels can be printed because of its built in feature. It is integrated to digital libraries because of micro docs built in.

Library bulletin can be generated. Built in new clippings manager. Records can be downloaded from other libraries through internet. Records can be exported to CSV files, MARC 21, MARC XML,ISO-2709,Excel and MS Access file. It provides digital repository of full text articles, news and book chapters which can be searched through internet Z39.50 servers. Software is provided free of cost to libraries with free upgradation, training and support. But only government libraries can get free software. e-Granthalaya 4.0 version is available in National Informatics centre cloud for Government libraries only on request basis with free hosting of application and databases. An official letter can be sent to e-Granthalaya to get access to e-Granthalaya 4.0 online account duly signed by the User authority. The request form can be downloaded from NIC. It entertains only group request which means individual college or organization cannot get access. The head of the group organizations like polytechnics in the state can submit request to DG (NIC) from Directorate of Technical Education which is a parent organization. Individual school/college /polytechnics request will not be entertained.

Building of union catalogue is free i-e by hosting of catalogues in NIC server in as a shared database. Free home page for each library is allowed. Changing and up dation policy is on the basis of feedback from the client libraries. The changes made in software or technological improvements will be informed to user libraries and they can migrate their existing version to the new upgraded version as per their instructions. For updates the users can visit *http:// egranthalaya.nic.in* and union catalogue is available at *http:/ /wwweGLibNet.Gov.in*. The e-Granthalaya 1.0 first released in 2003 aimed to meet the requirements of Public libraries and it is called Public Libraries version. In the year 2005 – version 2.0 was released which focused government libraries and it is called as Government Libraries edition. In the year 2007 – version 3.0 made it a network edition whereby local/ LAN database and remote/WAN database connectivity was provided. In the year 2015 version 4.0 enterprise edition of e-Granthalaya was released which made it a web based edition and enabled government libraries to have web based/ cloud ready application hosted in NIC. The highlight of 4.0 Enterprise edition is a centralised database for all the libraries under one department

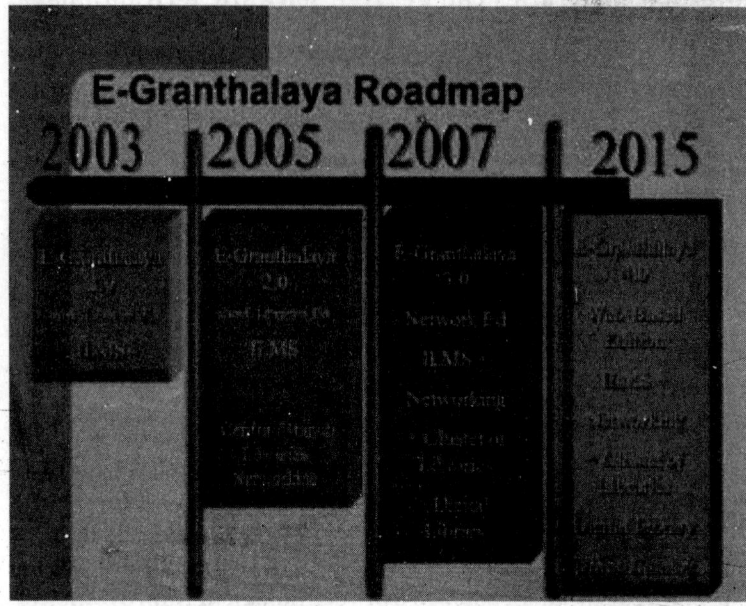

Fig. 6.20. Different versions of e-Granthalaya.

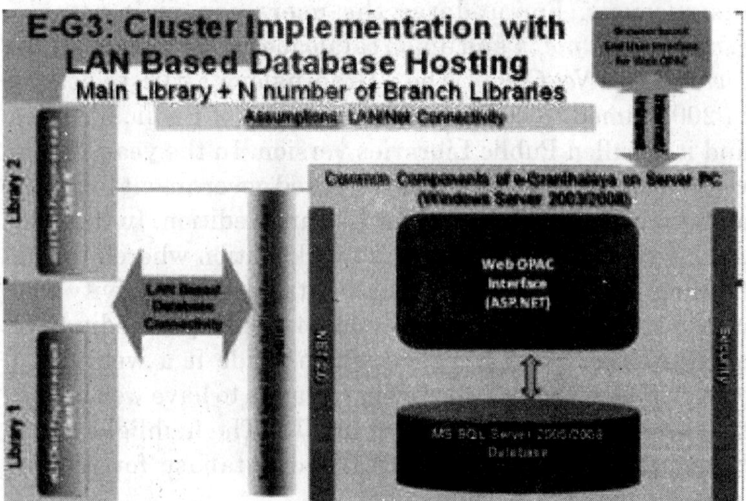

Fig. 6.21. LAN based e-Granthalaya

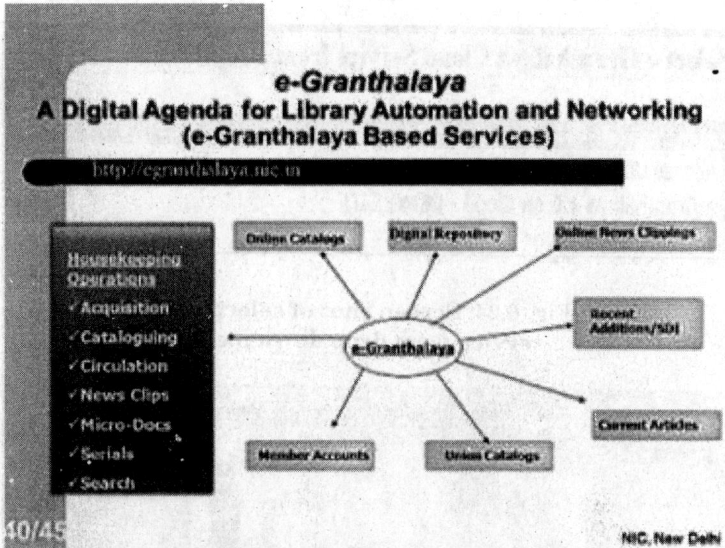

Fig. 6.22. An overview of e-Granthalaya supporting features

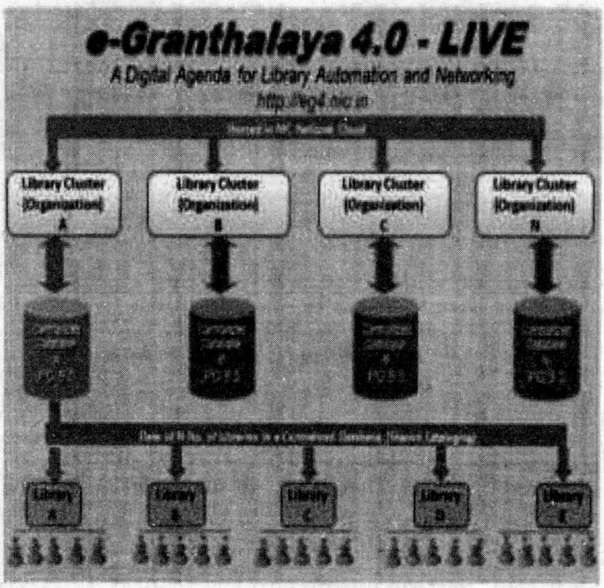

Fig. 6.23. Screen shot of e-Granthalaya 4.0 version

Fig. 6.24. Screen shot of selecting a service from drop down menu

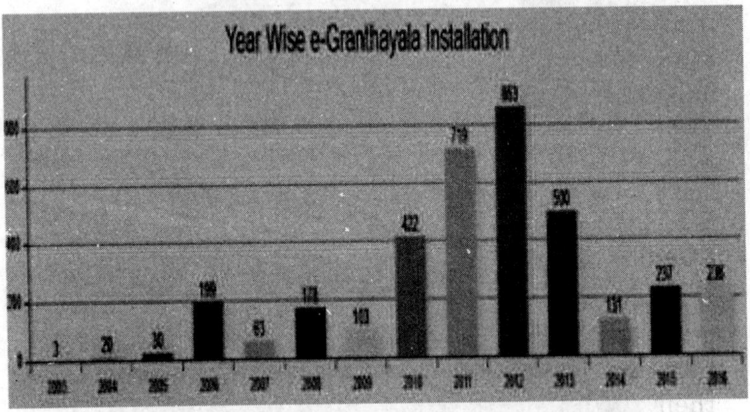

Fig. 6.25. e-Granthalaya yearwise installation in libraries

The important developments of version 4.0 are based on NET.4.0 Providing ASP.NET application. Built in APIs (application program interface) for external services like google/amazon/LOC. Reports are possible in different formats such as pdf/doc/html. It has integration with open source PostgreSQL DBMS and with MSSQL server. Manages metadata for non- book materials including legal documents. For implementation of eG3 version there are paid options for data entry and training or getting CD of software from NIC which can be run and maintained by the library itself without cost, getting online support from NIC. NIC offers e-mail, phone support for any problems. NICs paid services are onsite training, installation, one month support, hundred sample records, data entry, data migration, manpower deployment, website design and hosting. In eG3 components front end data entry programs (windows forms) are installed in each client PC. MS-SQL server 2005 back end database is installed on server PC. Web forms are installed on server PC. Granth service a web service for remote database connectivity is installed on server PC. e-Granthalaya software will be placed in NIC server from where it can be installed automatically on the client PC. Updating feature also can be downloaded automatically when the application is run on the client PC every time. Latest version 4.0 is a "cloud ready application" which helps in web based data entry solution in enterprise mode containing a centralised database for cluster of libraries. PostgreSQL an open source DBMS is used as a back end for database solution in e-Granthalaya 4.0 version.

6.3. LIBRARY INTEGRATED MANAGEMENT SYSTEM - COMPARISON OF SOFTWARE

Comparative study of ILMS software and critical evaluation is essential for the selection of software for librarians to implement automation in their libraries as per their requirements. The comparative features are briefly listed.

General Features

Koha and New Genlib provide source code for configuration and customization. They involve user community for the developments of their products.

Libsys and Virtua do not provide source code, but all the vendors update the software from time to time following international standards for metadata interoperability and also understanding the customization requirements of the client libraries. All Integrated Library Management Systems are user friendly in different aspects.

Koha in terms of installation, New Genlib with regard to functionality of modules. These offer service and provide support through their extensive documentation and tutorials. The commercial vendors Virtua and Libsys provide immediate support through Annual Maintenance Contract (AMC), which means that since they are commercial software and AMC's maintained, the contact persons are available for immediate support in case of any problem with regard to installation, training, to running reports or to provide additional customization for user benefit. At the time of installation at the client library they provide support and customization.

Koha is upgraded continuously by the Koha community.

Koha and Virtua facilitates various levels of access permission to staff members who can use the site, but in New Genlib and Libsys this functionality is lacking.

Koha is written in PHP and PERL where as New Genlib and Virtua are written in JAVA. Libsys uses C/C++ programming languages.

All the ILMS have application servers, web servers, and database servers and also backup facility in the event of loss of data, data security is ensured.

Browser compatibility through intranet and data migration is also featured. After installation support web based modules, customization, networking and standalone features are also possible in all the ILMS.

Digital library integration, with uploading/ downloading of Tiff etc documents. Soul 2.0 uses MS SQL as RDBMS, whereas e-granthalaya works on PostgreSQL. Libsys does not require to install RDBMS additionally because it is their proprietary product but has option to have the support of SQL server, or Oracle as back-end. All the software's provide RSS feeds, MARC 21 format following ISO-2709 for exchange of bibliographic data. SOUL and e-granthalaya is upgraded continuously and support client libraries for data migration, conversion and carrying out the updates. Libsys and Virtua send the entire new versions in the form of CD for installing.

Acquisitions

With regard to the acquisitions most of the processes are fulfilled in Libsys and Virtua. Electronic data interchange (EDI) feature is lacking in New Genlib, Similarly unicode editor is lacking in Koha and New book listing in New genlib. With regard to acquisitions, SOUL 2.0 supports authority files of personal names, generating reports of their choice and using templates. It is a simple budgeting system with different budget accounts. Order processing cancellation, reminders, receipts and payments are handled. Master files such as currencies, vendors, with report functions. Soul 2.0 produces accession register either sequentially or non-sequentially. Book suggestions are possible. e-Grandhalaya also provides authority files for authors, publishers, subjects and cross-checking. The work-flow for each module is designed as per the requirements of Indian libraries. This software also supports the printing of accession register, bill registers, and budget management with multiple budget heads. Other regular functions are included in this software.

Acquisition module of any software should provide main functions such as - budget maintenance, tracking of expenditure, knowing the balance amount, transfer of funds, etc.

Reports

Virtua supersedes report function in all aspects but reports are not provided at the module level. It is provided at Info Station portal where templates for Acquisition, New book lists, Cataloguing, Serials control, Circulation Account summaries and OPAC are available. They can be customized, saved and reports can be run as per their requirements.

New Genlib and Libsys lack certain types of report like order card slips. New Genlib lacks report of order status, request status and fund status. Libsys lacks certain types of reports. But Libsys 7 latest version provides some customizable reports. Virtua satisfies reporting function at large. Libsys has options to modify process and quit at every module making it easier to work with. Some reports are featured at the module level itself.

Claims for unsupplied items can easily be sent from Koha, New Genlib and Virtua and Libsys.

Both the Soul 2.0 and e-Granthalaya software have an exhaustive provision for generating statistical, customizable and other reports..

Cataloguing Module

All the ILMS packages are compliant with the latest standards such as Z39.50 client and server data interchange, copy cataloguing using Z39.50 and retro conversion.. Printing catalogue in MARC format and 856 tag with sub field u for cataloguing web resources are also featured in all ILMS. Barcode generation is also fulfilled. List of new catalogue cards are not featured in New genlib. Soul 2.0 supports multi-lingual database for Indian and foreign languages and it is UNICODE based. It follows international standards such as MARC21, AACR II and MARC XML. Soul 2.0 provides platform for bibliographic database such as MySQL, Ms-SQL or any other RDBMS. Supports online copy cataloguing from MARC21 formats. Provides different template for data entry of different type of documents. Provides cataloguing of e-resources. Supports stock verification, book bank, vigorous maintenance functions and with enhanced security at transactional level. It is compliant to ISO 2709 standard for data exchange. e-grandhalaya supports 15 regional languages, with UNICODE compliance. Module-wise permissions to software users, with full cataloguing and retro-conversion facility. It supports multi volume and multi copy. Provides facility for downloading records from internet. Export records in .csv /.txt / MARC21 /MARC.xml /ISO2709 / MS access / XMLformats. Merger of databases into single database. Common centralised database for all libraries under one organization, thereby the data redundancy can be avoided. Main and branch libraries share acquisition and cataloguing functions. It can generate bibliography in AACR format.

Serials Control

863 holdings tag for enumeration and chronology is available in Koha and Virtua only. Libsys do not support adding supplements and indexes, whereas New Genlib supports this features.

Virtua serials module is not so compatible to support approval process for renewals for the current year subscription from the previous year. Whereas it is designed in a more compatible way in Koha and Libsys. Serial module not so compatible in New Genlib.

Soul serial module has following functions – suggestions, master database, loose issues check-in, payments, reminder, binding and title history. There is provision for exporting and importing data by using ISO 2709 exchange format. Similar to Libsys software, Soul also has provision for article indexing for journals and book chapters. It supports cataloguing of e-resources. e-granthalaya has provision for subscription auto scheduling and monitoring of the issues. It manages e-books with digital files in PDF and other formats providing e-book viewer. Library picture or logo can be uploaded. It manages metadata for non-book material including legal documents. It has built-in data entry statistics.

Circulation Module

Soul maintains up to date membership records. status of collection, transaction history of patrons and default patrons etc. 'Set library' feature is not found in New Genlib and Libsys. Tracking the in house cataloguing feature is lacking in New Genlib. In processing book locations are not possible in New Genlib and Libsys. Bindery management is lacking in Koha. Patron's loan history and most checked out or patrons with no check out are not found in New Genlib. Average loan item is lacking in New Genlib. Overdue collection is lacking in Libsys. Book status and book history is not seen in New Genlib. Short term loan is not seen in Koha.

RFID solutions are compatible with all the ILMS. The circulation module of SOUL and Libsys7 is fully compliant with the NISO Circulation and Interchange Protocol (NCIP) version 2 for electronic surveillance. Item status is maintained with various reports. e-Granthalaya supports smart multipurpose cards with photo facility. It integrates the main and branch library functions.

Web OPAC

WebOPAC offer different types of searches such as basic/advanced using Boolean operators and truncation, parenthesis search, Proximity search etc. Complete search options are available in Libsys and Virtua. Libsys provides facility to link multimedia file attachments which can be viewed through OPAC meeting the requirements of certain specific libraries.

Search and retrieval process with publisher name, publisher place, series are present in Koha and Libsys. Koha and New Genlib offer searches through call number. Libsys provides search through publication date, accession number etc. Virtua offers LCCN, ISSN and Imprint and all other search options.

Virtua provides searches of all types. Search results can be shortened by applying parameters such as - publication date, format, language, year, nature of content, place of publisher are found in Virtua. Hypertext links in the bibliographic record display is offered through author or title in all the ILMS.

Call number search is also supported by most of the ILMS-Koha and Libsys. Current Awareness Service is available in New Genlib and Virtua, Libsys and e-Granthalaya. SDI is present in all the six ILMS. The data import/export function is found to be a common feature in all the software's.

Soul has simple and advanced as well as Boolean features with minimum keying in information. It enables displaying and downloading of records with MS excel, PDF and MARC XML. Search facilitates acquisition status of the item. e-Granthalaya has built-in Z39.50 client search and also built-in search module that supports basic and advanced search. It supports a feature of CAS / SDI services and documentation work. It is regularly updated with enhanced features. It is designed to provide built in service for full text news clipping. The exhaustive web based OPAC interface is providing separate membership modules.

6.4. CONCLUSION

Currently SOUL is the highly preferred software by University libraries. SOUL 1.0 began in 2000 and SOUL 2.0 was released in January 2009.Many other libraries are shifting towards open source software like Koha and NewGenlib if they have computer skills personnel in their libraries. Even the INFLIBNET made visits across the country and found that only 35% of the state funded Universities and Colleges in urban areas have automated library applications. In rural areas and in public libraries so far the computer facilities are not available. However, in the metropolitan cities like Delhi, Mumbai, Kolkata, Chennai, Ahmedabad, Bangalore, Chandigarh, Hyderabad, Noida and Pune 90%to100% academic libraries are automated.

7

User Interface, The Web OPAC (Automation of User Services)

7.1. INTRODUCTION

The OPAC is an effective tool as it is the only module that users can access and use for their interaction with the library staff, resources and services. It is an online catalogue that enables browsing, speedy searching of library database for locating books, journals, periodicals and manuscripts in a library or in groups of libraries. The books or reading materials are arranged according to the subject content that is classified according to a scheme of classification code e.g. DDC classification and the internal classification subsystem in catalogue uses MARC-21 standard format with the call number, which facilitates web OPAC users to search into library database. In one word, the OPAC can be termed as user interface of library database. The OPAC terminals are though made available in the central hall of the library or nearby the reading/stack halls for library visitors, the web OPAC can be accessible worldwide by the distant users also. OPAC database can be accessed by a single key word at the click of the mouse or used applying advanced search facility with Boolean operators or filters to refine the results. The search results are helpful in getting complete detail of the document related to search query, saving the time of the researchers.

7.2. BASIC CHARACTERISTICS OF THE OPAC

- User interface helps users to enter their search requests and permits the user to view the results that are retrieved and navigate their search among the hits until they get refined results. The navigation between hits and across related records with help of hyperlinks is the most advantageous feature in most of the web based OPACs.
- Backend integrated database of the library and in some cases authority files can also be invoked with the key board while conducting the search.
- Functionality Feature helps users in searching, viewing and downloading the records. This search and display functions are possible because of the underlined database engine consisting of Relational Database Management System (RDBMS). It has the query language index files with display and reporting feature.
- Online Help facility: It allows users to make effective use of the OPAC.

7.3. WEB OPAC

It is accessible through internet and provides access to the library's bibliographic database by means of terminal or PC, search results is readily in understandable form, provides remote access from the library's location, information about events , links to circulation files, reference help etc. Various access points such as author, title, keywords, subjects, periodical title, class numbers, series, ISSN,ISBN etc are provided. Using hypertext links navigation is possible through bibliographic record. It can link to the full text if it is available.

7.3.1. Difference between OPAC and Web OPAC

OPAC can be accessible in the intranet environment with the local area network facility and hence it is limited to that group. And users have to adhere to the program of the particular software in that library whereas Web OPAC is accessible globally from anywhere. Web OPAC uses html files with hyperlinks to the subject areas.

7.3.2. Advantages of Web OPAC

It is accessible globally all the time. Status of the book can be known to the staff and the user. Reprint request can be sent to the users by email. There is no space and time constraint for searching any documents. Anybody can search any document belonging to not only this library but any other network library.

7.4. SEARCH AND DISPLAY FEATURES OF WEB OPACS

Web OPAC expose search functionality, through two broad approaches, viz Basic Search and Advanced Search. The basic search is also called as simple search and the advanced search is also called as guided or power search.

The basic search : This search allows the users to select a single search field with a key word. For example the author or creator keywords enable the users browse the list of authors and chose author's name. Once the users' select the search term and a search is executed, the display and other functionalities of OPAC come into play. A user can specify the number of pages that they would like to view in the web OPAC search results. In the search results, brief content of the records will be displayed in the first appearance with few fields with hyperlinks to the full text or full text sources. It may even direct users to other related records viz. by the same author or same publisher or same subject. Each record shows the physical location of the item along with a link to location of electronic resources, that is - the table of contents or images of the displayed item, which could be a PDF text file or Image file. Some OPACs allow the users to select the field that they wish to se e in the retrieved display i.e. author or title or publisher etc. Some OPACs makes the sorting provisions according to relevance to the search query or publication date whether new or old.

Advanced Search : Advanced search facilitates several options for searching the information.

- In this number of terms can be combined
- The term as a phrase can be searched. Ex: 'Library Management'
- Any of these terms may be present i.e. 'Libraries' or the term 'Management or both may be present in the titles even if the titles are not adjacent to each other using AND or NOT Boolean operator.
- All of these terms can be present i.e. search for all the items in which the titles have both library and management
- Web OPAC should be up to date without errors as it is displayed worldwide.
- Google generation of today demand freedom to tag items of their interest.

The main difference between card catalogue and OPAC are that it is more user centric and it provides more access points for eg' search through ISBN, ISSN and keywords etc. We can say that it provides access to each and every part of bibliographic record so that users can find data using keyword searching contained in notes including content notes. OPACs usually provide author, title, subject heading, call numbers, ISBN, ISSN and keyword search. In many academic libraries OPACs provide other access points such as government document numbers, music numbers, reserved book list by courses or by instructor etc. Broadening or narrowing the search through Boolean operators, AND or NOT in the OPAC. They can also refine their search results by language data publication, type of document which is not found in card catalogue. OPAC is the means of interaction between the user and the library. Web OPAC is an independent program that is designed separately from the library program. It is programmed in such a way that helps users to access the OPAC through their own way of searching for the ease of borrowing. They can also request for the information about the borrowing and can also make automatic reservation for the book.

7.5. EVOLUTION OF OPAC

- First generation of OPACs had limitations. They were programmed to use command such as "a" for author, "t" for title etc. by an exact string of characters that would be matched against the systems internal index. They were highly intolerant of user mistakes. There was no browsing title and no keyword searching and no Boolean operators. They were similar to card catalogue.
- Second generation of OPAC from the late 1980s had greater improvements over the first generation and had greatly improved the user interface with the use of keyword searching Boolean operators thereby increasing the number of access points for searching. It supported truncation wild card and browsing capabilities and provided greater manipulation of search results. Nowadays web OPACs are compliant with graphical user interface and Z 39.50 features.
- Next generation online library catalogue: Library 2.0 is extension of web 2.0 of library services providing effective user services such as community participation and feedback thus offering possibilities for online social networking. OPAC 2.0 with the application of web 2 online catalogues can be termed as the next generation OPAC 2 enabling more clearer catalogue functionality through the new features by bringing refining options to the results screens like narrowing by call number range, by subject topic , brief view and full view and sort by relevance. Some provide discovery options such

as related search terms spelling variants and translations, sort options. Some others provide related subject headings broken down by subdivision, provides suggestions to search by related author or subject, and date clustering. Accessing to information by one's own familiar tags or those of peers in a social network.

- Application of web 2.0 technologies in Libraries such as Blogs, Wikis, Podcasts, and RSS feeds, instant messaging, social networking etc are the services that the users expect to interact. These applications make it more user centric and user interfaced in the digital era.
- OCLC offers WorldCat.org local, a discovery and delivery interface for use by library or library consortium. It allows libraries to combine the metadata of OCLC member libraries worldwide and customize WorldCat.org for local discovery and delivery. It features faceted browsing, cover art, and a multilingual interface, as well as customised relevancy ranking. Libraries can apply their own local branding and Information.

7.6. USER'S EXPECTATIONS IN THE CHANGING INFORMATION ENVIRONMENT

User's requirements and expectations are the key to development of any system. Some of the user's expectations of being part of the library system by involving themselves and carrying out certain operations without being in queues and also searching as well as use behaviors that have posed challenges to library management systems.

- Users expect large amount of freedom in managing their access to information.
- Users want access to not only library resources but also other types of material available on the web
- Users want not only simple search interface that is easy to use but also retrieves items ranked by relevance

and points to related items, reviews, recommendations and allows a degree of faceted searching.

- Users want to access all the full text documents and all the digital content through the Library management system.
- Google generation of today demand freedom to tag items of their interest, access to information by their own tags or those of peers in a social network.
- Users prefer to view the latest arrivals of books, journals and other material, apart from browsing, navigating and searching.
- Users would like to send their recommendations for the purchase of books and other material for the library.
- Library patrons prefer to receive alerts about the receipt of recommended books, preferred journals and return of reserved book/s
- Users expect to receive alerts or notifications about overdue books/journals borrowed by them
- Patrons would anticipate to self-register into the library system, upload their picture or image and get integrated to academic/administrative divisions.
- Users demand for renewing books online without visiting the library
- Users would prefer to self-check-in and checkout without waiting in long queues.
- Further, users would like to know the status of book or journal, whether recommended, ordered, received, in-process, checked out, available, in-bindery, missing or damaged, written off etc.
- In view of the e-commerce applications, after receiving email notifications library users may even prefer to transact the overdue or loss of book charges online from their bank or credit card accounts and get the dues cleared.

The WWW and graphical user interface has made web-based OPACs largely accepted by the users. Web–based OPAC's enable users to access information from any local or remote corner of the world through internet facility thereby providing easy and convenient access to the OPAC.

7.7. AUTOMATION OF USER SERVICES:

In automation environment, web OPAC obviously is the result of the entire library integrated operations and gateway to library/s resources. Over the period and generations, it is being designed and developed as the focal point of entire library operations and also the interface through which the users can trigger the library operations and interact with the library and also become part of the refinement of library services by integrating the Web 2.0 technologies, mobile applications and interactive applications available through LIS packages.

- Integration of web 2.0 technologies such as Blogs, Wikis, Podcasts, and RSS feeds, instant messaging, social networking etc. to library web OPACs have made OPACs more user centric and enable users to interact with the library. The following screenshot illustrates the sharing of user's feedback or opinions through web 2.0 tools integration to library web OPAC.
- As the internet Wi-Fi is connected to smaller devices like mobile phones, tablets, notebooks, laptops etc. the increasing mobile applications have been drawing the attention of publishers and LIS vendors to device the e-resources and OPACs websites also mobile friendly in order to provide seamless access to web OPACs. So that the users with smart phones can to access web-OPAC and be in touch with library all the time.
- The VTLS software through "Mobile Chamo" phone applications provides access to Web OPAC in their smart phones.

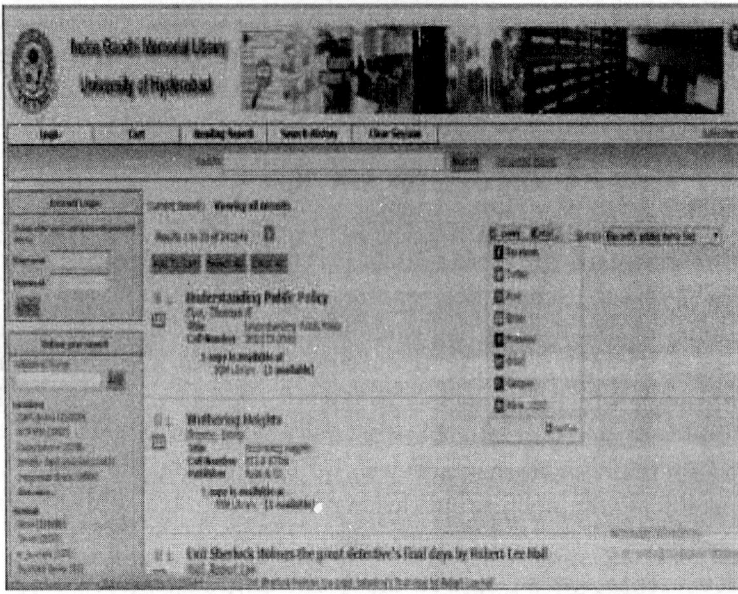

Fig. 7.1. Screen shot of VTLS Web OPAC - Chamo

- The Dublin Core Metadata standards for cataloguing the Internet resources has paved way to add internet resources to the OPAC and provide value added services of web OPAC to the users.
- The future Web OPACS using Google interface will be able to provide much more functionalities.

Obviously the automation of integrated library operations is the solution in designing the Web OPAC more effective as it depends on the structure and design of the relational database that holds the data, the input and also the LIS application software that helps to manipulate the records. The next generation library OPACs are designed to meet most of the expectations of library users and their preferences.

- Acquisition system receives the recommendations for books, journals and other material, checks for duplication, place order for a specified location, receives the copy/copies and sends for technical processing.

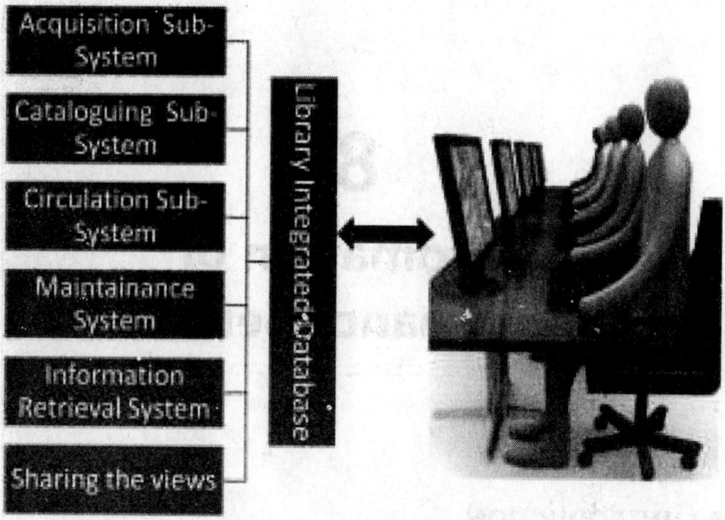

Fig. 7.2. User Interface – Users Accessing Library Integrated Database

- Cataloguing processes the material according to the latest MARC21 format with specification of language, form, format, type of material, publisher, publication country, location, year of publication and also the URL. The detailed specifications in cataloguing system enables to execute filters in OPAC that can be applied to refine the search results and achieve precision in retrieval.
- Circulation system create settings for loan period, lead period, overdue charges per day, maximum number of notices to be served and number of renewals. These settings may vary as per the type of patron and also the type of material, which can be circulated.
- Maintenance system enables to manage the status of library material and also be able to modify the status of an item from available to missing or in-bindery or even turn to non-circulatory etc.

8

Automation of Maintenance Services

8.1. INTRODUCTION

Libraries and information centres are involved in the acquisition of information material, their organization and maintenance. In this process, every library has its own policies, procedures, manuals, files and registers. They help in managing the library systematically. Apart from attending to user queries, libraries need to maintain statistics and answer to the administration, finance as well as audit of the parent organization with data and also the higher bodies in the hierarchy. Further they need to respond to with other organizations sharing some information in the form of surveys or correspondence.

8.2. PRE-AUTOMATION MAINTENANCE RECORDS

During pre-automation times, libraries usually maintain the files related to approvals, orders, invoices and payments and audit files, staff personal files, library committee, stock verification, weeding and write off orders etc. The big libraries maintain the following registers for the purpose of permanent records, statistics, and for any verification compulsorily.

1. Visitors register
2. Indents register
3. Accession register
4. Periodicals register / kardex
5. Registers to note the refunds of missing issues or non-receipts
6. Staff Attendance register
7. Bills register/s
8. Stock register of non-consumables
9. Stock register of consumables
10. Members registers
11. Books/periodicals Issues/returns or tickets
12. Registers for the amount collected and deposited towards overdue charges or loss of books or any other penalties
13. Stock verification, missing books for write off
14. Lists of damaged books for write off

Manuals are helpful for standardization of processes pertaining to each section of the library – library administration, acquisition of material, cataloguing, serials and circulation, user services and stack maintenance etc. They contain the details of the international as well as national standards to be followed involving processes, deviations as per the local requirements, library committee recommen-dations, and modifications etc.

8.3. LIBRARY MAINTENANCE IN AUTOMATION ENVIRONMENT

The automation eased not only the in-house operations, facilitated user services but also generate lot of data required for statistical purpose and to provide information to the administration and finance of the parent organization, in the form of reports either through respective sub-modules or a separate reports module. Most of the reports are generated out of the library integrated operations but to derive some status reports by updating with necessary data that need to be input in the respective bibliographic records. For example recommended, approved, ordered, received, in-process, available, checked-out, in bindery etc. statuses are found, whereas certain statuses like 'damaged', 'withdrawn' or 'weeded out' or written off or 'lost the book in circulation' have to be noted & updated in the system.

Several registers can be generated through Library integrated operations. Primarily the acquisition operations

1. Recommendations register
2. Accession register
3. Periodicals register / kardex
4. Registers to note the refunds of missing issues or non-receipts
5. Bills register/s
6. Vendors register

Similarly circulation section can retrieve

1. Members registers
2. Registers for the amount collected and deposited towards overdue charges or loss of books or any other penalties
3. Loss of books in circulation register

Administration or Maintenance section can generate the registers by updating the items of bibliographic records with relevant statuses – 'missing', 'damaged books' and 'written off' etc.

Several files and statistical reports also can be generated from the acquisition, circulation operations of the library such as –approvals, orders, bills, payments, order cancellations, non-receipts, refund files and the statistical reports like library acquisitions by year, budget head, recommending department, vendor and subject etc.

From the journals check-in and cataloguing of books

and other material, it is possible to generate lists for display in new arrivals as well as to maintain their counts for statistical and audit purpose.

Majority of the LIS application software are facilitating the data output in the respective sub-modules or through customizable reports module.

8.4. MAINTENANCE FUNCTIONS IN LIS APPLICATION SOFTWARE

Some software are provided with sub-modules for these maintenance operations such as bindery, stack rectification, stock verification. Stock verification /rectification can be carried out manually noting down the call number or accession number on library records or can be done with the help of barcode readers or by using RFID technologies to identify the missing books in the stacks. However, status files generated from the Library database reveal the various statuses of books those are not available in stacks.

The books should be properly arranged on the shelf call number wise. The status of the books should be shown in the OPAC whether it is issued, returned or sent for binding so that the user's time is not wasted in searching for the books. If the book is lost or damaged, it should also be shown in the OPAC. In an open access system there is bound to be misplacement or loss of books which has to be checked periodically. The main stock record of the library is its catalogue which are the keys to the library stock arranged in a systematic order.

The Stock need be verified as part of its audit purposes. Many libraries in the western countries have abandoned stock verification as they found it to be costlier than the amount spent for it. But in Indian environment with open access there is bound be misplacement or loss which has to be rectified and loss of books has to updated in the system so that the web OPAC shows the correct status of the book so stock verification can be done as part of rectification and also for audit purposes. It is not mandatory to conduct every year but once in five years the total collection has to be verified but again it depends upon the availability of the man power and cost involved. An example of Libsys software stock verification function is explained in an automated environment.

In Libsys Initiate Stock Verification function from cataloguing sets the system for stock inventory process which should be run only once during the cycle of stock verification.

In Stock Verification function the system is set to accept accession numbers one by one, registering in the database the presence of the item on the shelf. On entering an accession number and pressing the enter key, the system displays brief details of the title along with its current status.

This sub-menu has three options Modify, Quit and Process.

- 'Modify option' is selected to change the status of the book(Default is 'on shelf) to either of the Damaged or Withdrawn
- The 'Quit option is selected for accepting another accession number.
- The 'Process' option is selected for registering the presence of the book on the shelf.

There is also a facility to accept the list of accession numbers in a file, where each line contains only one accession number. This is helpful in grouping titles having the same status, for example 'Withdrawn Books'. In such a case file option may be used. The file of accession numbers is developed off-line and is saved in a file which is used as the input file when the system asks for the file name.

On entering the above information and pressing the enter key, the system will start registering accession numbers for verification in the database.

Verification Report function provides a list of all the books either alphabetically or by accession number or class number. There is a facility to include the status against each title.

- On Display
- On Shelf
- Checked-out
- Lost/Written-off
- Damaged
- Bindery
- Withdrawn
- Missing
- In-Process
- Reference

Reports may be generated separately for any of the above groups. One may also select any one or more groups to be included in one report. There is also an option to specify "Location", in case the verification reports are needed for specific collections.

In Virtua the list of call numbers can be generated and checked in the stack area by checking the presence of the item and simultaneously in the system the status can be updated either on shelf, check out, Lost / written off / damaged / withdrawn, missing, in Process, Reference etc.

After stock verification the report has to be maintained by updating the status of the items in the automated system so that user will know the exact status of the items in the library .Loss of books file can be maintained in the system and every year the same list can be checked and misplaced books can be traced and updated in the system.

Similarly weeding should be dealt when the collection is increasing. In order to maintain library collection up to date as per the organizational priorities and users requirements, it is necessary to weed out certain material to get stack space for new additions and to avoid clogging in the services. Thus, the library collection needs to be evaluated in terms of its significance, use and the current nature of content drawing criteria for weeding the library material. It is essential to frame clear cut policies for evaluating, weeding the library material and also documenting the policies by developing manuals. Further the acquisition and catalogue records of the library are to be updated with necessary information required for users and administration regarding the changes made in collection. It should be reported to the audit section.

The users access online databases and the usage statistics are provided by the publishers which can be downloaded and preserved for audit purposes. This can also serve as Return on Investment (ROI) to justify the renewal of the databases for the current year and to know the research output of the user community thereby justifying the subscription to online databases.

8.5. COMPACT BOOK STACK SHELVING

At present users and in future users come to the library not for borrowing but for discussing in groups and relying on libraries for library services and technology to apply for jobs and studying alone. The libraries are faced with space constraint and going in for Library Rolling Stack Shelving or *compact book stacks on rails system* to enable libraries to reduce the space that are currently used to store books and gain space to meet their users'. The Compact Book Stacks on Rails System Stores More Than Conventional Shelving. This is a modern method of compact stacks to store library materials.

The system consists of shelving that is mounted on wheeled carriages attached to a rail system anchored to the floor. In this system fixed aisles are not required between every stack. The stacks can be compressed into a smaller space and a single aisle is created as needed by rolling the stacks apart to access a specific range. Motorized drive system is used for moving the stacks. The Library Rolling Stack Shelving can hold approximately three times as many books as conventional shelving in the same floor area.

Fig. 8.1. Compact Book Stack Shelving

It can store Videos, CDs, and DVDs, Newspapers and periodicals, Oversize materials like maps and drawings, Archival boxes, Artwork collections etc. When all the materials are not shelved in such shelves there is a need to maintain such collection with necessary location status for easy access to the books. In view of automation the materials so kept in such areas need to be incorporated in the catalogue holdings indicating the status so that users can themselves pick up books from such shelves. In some libraries because of the open access system when such shelves are used only for shelving some reading material the same has to be indicated in the spine and also in the bay guides. some library they use these shelves for preserving passive collection.

Along with automation of house- keeping operations, the automation of managerial services help in maintaining the library with proper administrative functions and providing the necessary timely data to the authorities. This timely updating of data ensures easy and smooth functioning of the library and stack services.

9

Conclusion

It is a fact that the automation of in-house operations has changed the dimension of libraries in all the aspects - its way of functioning, maintenance of data and rendering of services all over the world. Though these developments entered late in India, the benefits are encouraging all the libraries to implement to improve their functioning and provide quality services to their users. The automation of integrated library operations is not a task of a day or a year. It is a continuous process in terms of inputting the data, updating the hardware, software as well as networking features and also going ahead with latest standards of cataloguing, indexing, and formats.

UNDERSTANDING THE COLLECTION, DATA, RETRIEVAL

The success of library automation depends on selecting the right application software that suits to the library services and requirements especially the mission of the parent organization. The licenses need to be discussed at the time of purchase. Further it is necessary to check for the compatibility of the software while adopting updates in new formats. Before implementing library automation, it is essential to know about the mission of the parent organization, its environment, library in terms of their collection, data as well as the kind of users and their information needs and also the financial resources. Then only it is possible to choose the right application software for library automation.

STANDARD PRACTICES

Another important factor that influences the quality of library database is maintaining the uniformity, and consistency all through the operations. To achieve this libraries need to follow standard practices such as —

- Initially set the locations, type of material, form of the material, physical formats, languages, language codes, currencies, budget (account) codes, type of patrons, material that can be circulated, types of statuses etc.
- Authority files need to be maintained and followed while rendering the bibliographic data without spelling, transliteration, rendering variations.

While automation the staff entering the data should be careful as the software will not spellcheck. The rules for entering the articles should be adhered to as it reflects in OPAC, the search and retrieval system. Missing books, lost books and withdrawn books should be indicated in the catalogue during updating the catalogue so that users are not mislead. If Unicode character set is not followed then while entering language records in English the 008 fixed field should be changed to the name of the language so that even if records are displayed in English it will be listed in the original language like Hindi, Telugu or any other language so that the list of language books can be generated and displayed which helps the user in search and retrieval. It is needless to say that every entry whether accession number or call number or a copy number there should be standard procedures to follow and input the same in the respective modules while automating the various in-house operations. These decisions, local variations and standard procedures are required to be recorded for all the modules thus enabling to maintain a clean database which ultimately results in effective information retrieval. It is required to handle the bibliographic data while importing from external sources in MARC21 format so that the data elements of all the records will be placed in appropriate fields and sub-fields.

LIS PACKAGES & CUSTOMIZATION

The Administration Module of the Integrated Library Management system should provide facilities for customization of user profiles, permissions, and budget, year and currency parameters. Furthermore before choosing a software for library automation, it is advisable to look for the feasibilities of customization both from vendor side and also the customer library side.

At the time of installation testing should be done. All the modules functionality should conform to the manual operations.

Most of the software provide easy functioning of cataloguing module and also make sufficient provisions for circulation of library material. But most of the software do not fulfil all the requirements of the acquisition processes, especially the complex subscription/renewal processes of serials. In some packages, the entry of serials data through cataloguing module (Koha) / or serials module (virtua) will be available in same database and visible through same search interface under title. It requires utmost attention while differentiating the entry of serial holdings because each serial is unique in its history and holdings. The work-forms should be designed in a way that the staff can easily fill the record without much of coded information. Help menus should direct the staff for inputting the data without mistakes. Even a non –technical person should be able to enter the data easily.

Accounting and budget should reflect the status of the funds to produce to the audit or accounts department. Depending up on the collection and fund position one has choose the software suitable for their library

Fund transfer and booking of titles in different fund account should be possible. Amount spent for the previous year with carry over fund for this year or additional fund provided should be possible in account set up of the administration module. Staff performance report should be generated to know the work output of the staff.

Cancellation of orders or reissue of the order to the same vendor or different vendor should be possible. Data entry should be shared across all the modules so that there is no redundancy in data entry.

Search and retrieval should be possible by all types like material, publication date, language and advanced search with key words and Boolean operators. Users should be trained in the use of OPAC and online databases. Web 2.0 applications like, blogs, Wikis, Social networking, RSS feeds should be applied to provide value added service to the users.

Recent development in cataloguing is Resource Description Access (RDA) which already certain libraries have started using it for their current cataloguing workflow. It was released in June 2010.The Library of Congress has full implementation of RDA. OCLC has compiled a list of the resources that are available to adhere to RDA at the library. The items cover works done in OCLC to support implementation of RDA and resources available from American Library Association, Library of Congress and other sources. RDA is a standard for descriptive cataloguing providing help and guidelines for formulating bibliographic data. It is useful for all libraries and other cultural organizations like Museums and Archives. It is a successor of AACRII. All the guidelines are available in RDA tool kit on online subscription site and in print format. Maintenance of RDA is a collective responsibility of the three RDA publishers American Library Association (ALA), Canadian Library Association (CLA) and the Chartered Institute of Library Information Professionals (CLIP) in the UK and the Australian Committee on Cataloguing, the British Library, and the Canadian Committee on Cataloguing, Deutsche National Bibliothek and the Library of Congress (LOC).

According to wikipedia "The primary distinction between RDA and AACR is structural. RDA is organised based on the Functional Requirements for Bibliographic Records (FRBR). These principles identify both the 'user tasks', which a library catalogue should make possible, and a hierarchy of relationships in bibliographic data. Descriptions produced using the instructions of RDA are intended to be compatible with any coding schema, including the data environments used for existing records created under the AACR2 rules"

The libraries should slowly adapt to RDA so that the modern way of getting access to resources can be enjoyed by the users and the libraries.

Cataloguing of electronic resources will also help users to have easy access to full text.

TRAINING & DOCUMENTATION

Proper training and documentation is very important for using software whether it is open source or commercial. Manual should be made available online to refer the details of the software or to take guidance at the time of working with it, when there is a doubt. Local contact persons should be available for instant help and technical support whenever need arises to customer libraries.

Bibliography

1. Alan Manifold, (2000), "A principled approach to selecting an automated library system", Library Hi Tech, Vol. 18 No. 2 pp. 119 -130
2. Aswal, R.S: AACR2R with MARC21: Cataloguing practice for 21st Century. New Delhi,ESS ESS Publications,2005.
3. Butcher, R. (1993), "An overview of British Library automation at St Pancras", 'Program,' Vol. 27,No. 3, pp. 281-92.
4. Chelatayakkot,Veerankutty: Automated detection of procured titles in a book recommendation list. *Kelpro Bulletin* ,Vol,19,no1,June 2015.pg 103-109
5. Coward, R.E. (1977), "The British Library Bibliographic Services Division", in Saunders, W.L.(Ed.), British Librarianship Today, Library Association, London, pp. 109-35.
6. Haravu, L.J. (2010): Emerging initiatives in library management systems. In International Conference on Academic Libraries: vision 2020. New Delhi, Mittal publications. Pp.241-243.
7. Haravu, L.J: Library automation: Design,Principles and Practise. New Delhi, Allied Publishers,2004.
8. Harrod, L M, Harrod's Librarians Glossary of Terms Used in Librarianship Documentation and the Book

Crafts and Reference Books. Vermont: Gower, 1987 p.707.

9. Hunder, Eric: Computerised cataloguing. London: Binglee, 1985.
10. Kent,Allen (1989). Encyclopedia of libray and information science.V .44 kochar, (1998). R & Library automation.
11. Knight J. P.,. Brewerton, G. P. Cooper,J.L : Automating Library Stock Ordering from Reading Lists.*D-Lib Magazine* Volume 19,Number,3/,March/April 2013.
12. Kumar PSG: Computerization of Indian libraries New Delhi BR Publishing Corporation 1987.
13. Madhusudhan, Margam and Vikas Singh, (2016), “Integrated library management systems: comparative analysis of Koha, Libsys , NewGenLib, and Virtua”, The Electronic Library , Vol. 34 no.2
14. Mc.Cree, Mark: Theft in the Public Library: an investigation into levels of theft and the impact it has on both services and staff: a study submitted for the award of M.Phil. at the University of Sheffield, 2000.
15. Paul Pandian,M (2010) : RFID for Libraries : A practical Guide. Oxford, Chandos Publishing.
16. Pgunjobi,R A and Awoyemira R.A (2012) : library automation with Koha . Library Hitech News vol.29 no.3 pp12-15
17. Ranganathan, S R, Reference service. Bombay: Asia Publishing House, 1961, p. 61
18. Riaz, Muhammad: Library automation: an introductory text. Islamabad, EBSCO Subscription Services, 1991.
19. Sudarshan.K.N and Kumar R. P and Srivastava D, (1995). Education for librarianship in information age.
20. Suryanarayana, V.V. and Nagaratnamani, G. (2012): Web-based library and information services. In

Ramaiah, L.S., Veeranjaneyulu, K. and Sujatha, G. eds. : Next generation librarianship: strategies for change management. Hyderabad, B.S.Publications. Pp. 265-267

21. Tapas Kumar Ghosh K.C. Panda, (2011), "Automated serials control at the Indian Institutes of Technology: an overview", Program, Vol. 45 Iss 2 pp. 173 – 184
22. Uma,V. : E-RAMS: a developing tool for managing electronic resources.ISST Journal of Advances in Librarianship, Vol. 3 No.2, (July - December 2012), p.p. 83-88
23. Uma,V. and Yakub Ali : Web OPAC : A tool to show case Library's resources for Their effective use Conference on Development of Academic and Public Libraries, in Digital Era : trends and issues. Proceedings. Lucknow, Bharat Book Centre Publisher & Book Sellers, November 24-25,2013
24. Virtua Manual .48.0 version.
25. http://www.libsys.co.in/companyprofile_overview.html
26. http://www.libsys.co.in/download/libsys7_brochure.pdf
27. http://igmlnet.uohyd.ac.in:8000/old.html
28. http://igmlnet.uohyd.ac.in:8000/web_reports/cgibin/InfoStation.cgi?mod=reports_list&func=list&lang_code=en&filter
29. https://en.wikipedia.org/wiki/Server_%28computing%29
30. http://whatis.techtarget.com/definition/server
31. https://www.google.com/?gfe_rd=cr&ei=TTDmVqr6Nujt8wfxrKiwBw&gws_rd=ssl#q=server+console
32. http://www.webopedia.com/DidYouKnow/Hardware_Software/router_switch_hub.asp
33. https://www.google.com/search?q=images+of+hubs+switches+and+cable+in+a+networking
34. http://www.webopedia.com/TERM/A/application.html

35. http://dublincore.org/documents/2012/06/14/dcmi-terms/?v=terms
36. http://dublincore.org/
37. https://en.wikipedia.org/wiki/Dublin_Core
38. http://www.inflibnet.ac.in/soul/downloads/SOUL2.0.pdf
39. https://www.google.co.in/?gfe_rd=cr&ei=pS28VuqnHuvI8Aej6Y-4Cg&gws_rd=ssl#q=optical+ cable+ definition
40. https://www.techopedia.com/definition/23735/server-software
41. https://www.loc.gov/marc/96principl.html
42. http://www.ifla.org/publications/unimarc-formats-and-related-documentation
43. http://unicode.org/standard/WhatIsUnicode.html
44. https://en.wikipedia.org/wiki/Z39.50
45. http://www.libsys.co.in/offerings-libsys7.html
46. http://egranthalaya.nic.in/eG4_UserManual.pdf
47. http://egranthalaya.nic.in/eG4.aspx
48. http://egranthalaya.nic.in/
49. http://www.slideshare.net/rupak/egranthalaya-ilms
50. http://www.inflibnet.ac.in/soul/downloads/SOUL2.0.pdf
51. http://koha-tools.sourceforge.net/
52. http://www.southwestsolutions.com/library/library-rolling-stack-shelving-compactbook-stacks-on-rails-system